Song of the Lord

Gītā in Yoga-Vāsiṣṭha

Song of the Lord

Gītā in Yoga-Vāsiṣṭha

With the Commentary
Tātparya-Prakāśa
of
Ananda-bodhendra Saraswati

Swami Veda Bharati

PRINTWORLD
Publishers of Indian Traditions

AHYMSIN
Publishers

Cataloging in Publication Data — DK
[Courtesy: D.K. Agencies (P) Ltd. <docinfo@dkagencies.com>]

Vedabhāratī, *Swami*, 1933-2015, **author.**
Song of the lord : Gītā in Yoga-vāsiṣṭha : with the commentary Tātparya-prakāśa of Ananda-bodhendra Saraswati / Swami Veda Bharati.
pages cm
Includes passages in Sanskrit.
Reprint. Originally published: 2013.
Includes bibliographical references and index.
ISBN 9788124606902 (HB)
ISBN 9788124606919 (PB)

1. Yogavāsiṣṭha – Criticism, interpretation, etc. 2. Vedanta. 3. Advaita. I. Ānandabodhendrasarasvatī Vāsiṣṭhamahārāmāyaṇatātparyaprakāśa. English. II. Yogavāsiṣṭha. Selections. English. III. Title.

LCC BL1139.76.V43 2024 | DDC 181.48 23

ISBN: 978-81-246-0690-2 (HB)
ISBN: 978-81-246-0691-9 (PB)
First published in India in 2013
Reprinted in 2024

Printed and published by:
D.K. Printworld (P) Ltd.
Regd. Office : 'Vedaśrī', F-395, Sudarshan Park
(ESI Hospital Metro Station) New Delhi – 110015
Phones : (011) 4172 2626, 9871394815
e-mail : indology@dkprintworld.com
Web : www.dkprintworld.com

in association with

AHYMSIN Publishers
Swami Rama Sadhaka Grama (SRSG)
Virpur Khurd, Virbhadra Road
P.O. Pashulok, Rishikesh - 249 203 (Uttarakhand)
Phones: (0135) 245 3030
e-mail:<ahymsinpublishers@gmail.com>/<info@ahymsin.org>
Website: www.ahymsin.org

Acknowledgements

THE text of the *Bhagavad-Gītā* as found in *Yoga-Vāsiṣṭha* (*YV-BhG*) was translated perhaps around 1975 and lay in the attic of the Meditation Center in Minneapolis, USA. While looking through the boxes of other previous unpublished writings I came upon this work. The gaps in the commentary have been filled in and the translation itself has been refined. It has now been expanded with an introduction to *Yoga-Vāsiṣṭha* (*YV*) and appendices.

I am most grateful to

- Jan Brzezinski (Shri Jagadananada Das) for going over it to check the scholarly details of style and content in his usual acutely careful way with such texts.
- Pandit Chandramani at our Ashram in Rishikesh and Sanjay Kumar in Vancouver for providing much important information on the texts from time to time while I travelled and they did the research at short notice whenever asked.
- Nancy Belding (Vikshana), formerly of our Ashram in the Meditation Center, Minneapolis, USA, for formatting the typescript laboriously with deep attention to fine detail.
- Mrs Lalita Arya for reading through and giving her valuable advice on many important points.
- Roderich Wahsner for obtaining a number of reference works published in Germany.

I wish to acknowledge the love and compassion of my Gurudeva Swami Rama of the Himalayas who, among other forms of grace conferred, unblocked me and first gave me an *ādeśa* (command) in 1972 to start composing my books.

Above all, I present this humble effort to the *ṛṣis* the profundity of whose words has been here miserably diluted. May they still accept this effort of love and devotion to pass on their message of transcendence.

Swami Rama Sadhaka Grama
Pashulok, Rishikesh (Uttarakhand)

Swami Veda Bharati

Contents

Introduction

Christopher Chapple

THE *Bhagavad-Gītā* is one of the most beloved works of India's religious traditions. It employs one of the most central human activities — receiving advice from a cherished friend — as a literary device to teach a profound path through which one may negotiate life's tremendous challenges and difficulties. Arjuna, tortured by the prospect of a looming yet unavoidable war against his own relatives, freezes on the battlefield. He sees no good reason to carry on with the inevitable killing of his teachers, cousins, friends, and other relatives. He seeks counsel from a trusted friend and cousin, Kṛṣṇa, whom he has chosen to serve as his charioteer in battle. Through Kṛṣṇa's sound advice, he learns the ways of knowledge, action, and devotion. Through these forms of yoga he regains his stability and sets forth with new resolve to re-engage with the world and perform the necessary deeds. Arjuna's struggle serves as a paradigm for effective decision-making. He embodies the archetype of the sensitive hero, a warrior who plunges into battle not due to anger or greed but due to an abiding sense of duty and responsibility. He engages selflessly, beyond ego, after a long period of discernment and insight.

In the traditional *Mahābhārata* narration of this encounter, Kṛṣṇa overwhelms Arjuna's petty faintheartedness and selfish obsessiveness by demonstrating to Arjuna that all things in the world are not only inseparable from God, but that God, in the form of time, will render all forms formless. All manifestations are fleeting. Not only all soldiers, but all people eventually perish. By showing Arjuna the evanescent nature of life and by revealing himself, Kṛṣṇa, to be the warp and woof of all reality, Arjuna comes to his senses and rejoins the fray.

The *Yoga-Vāsiṣṭha* presents a slightly different narrative approach to the education of Arjuna. Vasiṣṭha, one of the original seven Vedic seers (*ṛṣis*), tells his version of the story to his pupil Rāma as if it would happen eventually in the remote future. We know from the first book of the *Yoga-Vāsiṣṭha*, titled Vairāgyam (dispassion), that Rāma has a moment very similar to that of Arjuna in the *Mahābhārata*. Rāma is a teenager who has fallen into a state of deep melancholy. The sage Viśvāmitra praises Rāma's insights into the ephemeral nature of worldly concerns, and knows that the young prince would benefit from deeper philosophical training. At his urging, Vasiṣṭha, another great sage, begins to teach him through telling a series of stories that undermine any attachment to the fixity of things-as-they-appear. Just as Kṛṣṇa helped broaden and deepen Ajruna's understanding, Vasiṣṭha instructs Rāma.

The book known as the *Mokṣopāya* or the *Yoga-Vāsiṣṭha* consists of more than sixty stories told by Vasiṣṭha to Rāma to help stabilize his mind and eventually prepare him for adult responsibilities. Whereas Kṛṣṇa teaches eighteen forms of yoga in the *Bhagavad-Gītā* in 700 verses, Vasiṣṭha tells these stories over the course of more than 28,000 verses, one of the world's most lengthy philosophical discourses. Toward the end of the narrative, Vasiṣṭha summarizes the *Bhagavad-Gītā* over the course of seven chapters, hoping that the lesson learned by Arjuna can also be instructive for his pupil, Rāma.

Though many verses in these chapters are directly quoted from the *Bhagavad-Gītā*, some pronounced differences must be noted. True to his enduring theme throughout the *Yoga-Vāsiṣṭha*, the author urges that the universe be seen as inseparable from pure consciousness, equating this state as the union of *ātman* and *Brahman*. Rather than naming Kṛṣṇa as supreme, he emphasizes that God must be seen in all things and that the only path to achieve this knowledge is to renounce all sense of separation, all sense of ego. Vasiṣṭha beautifully describes the path to liberation as requiring purposeful purification. He urges the exertion of human will over the deleterious effects of past karam (*vāsanās*). With profoundly poetic language, Kṛṣṇa, as narrated by Vasiṣṭha, instructs Arjuna on how to overcome his attachments, to see through the changes, beyond the drama, to the core reality of existence. All things arise in the mind due to the conditioning of the mind. With a purified mind, all things are possible. Arjuna arrives at this point of freedom, announcing:

> My delusion is gone; I have attained mindfulness by your grace, O infallible one; now I remain free of doubt; I shall act according to your will. — *Yoga-Vāsiṣṭha* VI.58.1

With his ignorance dissolved, Arjuna takes up action once again on the battlefield of life.

This rendering by Swami Veda Bharati brings to light this important and unique version of the encounter between Kṛṣṇa and Arjuna. In the philosophy of the *Yoga-Vāsiṣṭha*, the ultimate is portrayed as universal and omnipresent. Rather than emphasizing the divine personhood of Kṛṣṇa, Vasiṣṭha teaches that all things in the universe must be seen as markers around an inclusive spaciousness rendered meaningful by consciousness. Swami Veda's delicate translation brings to the reader a sense of freedom, the space of pure consciousness (*cid-ākāśa*). Just as Arjuna learns of his true nature from this dialogue with Kṛṣṇa, so also the reader of this new translation will catch a glimpse of the beauty and the soaring possibilities of freedom. Freedom is to be discovered not by rejecting the world, but, in the words of Kṛṣṇa, by knowing that the true self neither is born nor does it die (52.36), allowing the eye to see, the ear to hear, the skin to touch, the tongue to taste in a state free from attachment (53.6), ready and willing to act within the world in accord with *dharma*.

Swami Veda's lucid translation encapsulates the message of Kṛṣṇa (and Vasiṣṭha) as follows: unrelenting thoughts (*vṛtti*) prevent the soul from seeing its true nature and sully the soul's perception of the world. By overcoming all past conditioning (*vāsanā*) and realizing the all-pervasive nature of pure consciousness, one can find freedom to act in a manner free from attachment, for the betterment of one's self as well as the world. By choosing to highlight the story of Arjuna from two sources, Swami Veda has melded together the wisdom of two great literary epics, the *Gītā* and the *Yoga-Vāsiṣṭha*, providing the reader with unparalleled access to the great truths and insights of yoga.

A Lyrical Metaphysical Epic

YOGA-VĀSIṢṬHA (*YV*) is the most lyrical philosophical text of the world. No matter how many translations or paraphrases of this incredibly rich text may be composed they cannot reveal all its depths. These depths can be explored and discovered only (1) by having access to the complex beauty of Sanskrit language and (2) by delving deep into a personal experience of the detailed and methodical processes of Vedāntic contemplations (*manana* and *nididhyāsana*) and yogic meditations (*dhyāna* and *samādhi*).

The text consists of gushing outpourings of the experiences of both the universal and the transcendent. The outpourings are the results of the *ṛṣis* — Vālmīki and Vasiṣṭha — and all others referred to in the *YV* stories, diving deep into the states, that are non-states, the very nature (*svabhāva*) of consciousness (*caitanya*).

It is impossible to list the contents of this text of 28,000+ verses (*ślokas*). *YV* does not belong to any one religious thought or a particular school of philosophy. It appears to syncretically combine the elements of different schools of Buddhism (primarily Vijñānavāda and Yogācāra), Jainism, Vedānta, Sāṅkhya, Śaiva Siddhānta (Tamil Śaivism), Kāśmīr Śaivism, Yoga, Tantra and many other spiritual resources but in our view it is a statement of its own philosophical system which is yet to be fully expounded in well-analysed categories.

It takes us on journeys in

- spaces within spaces and beyond spaces;
- time frames within time frames and beyond time frames.

YV makes us ponder over questions like:

> In which atom-mountain's cave, in which piece of stone are all the universes born and sustained?

These are answered in chapters like the ones leading us into the consciousness of *virāṭ-ātman*, the grand, majestic universe-person-self (6.II.19, 73-75, etc.).

In each of these space and time frames histories of universes and of empires, of sages and of the lost ignorant ones, of celestial beings (*deva*s) and of imaginary persons unfold, also as stories within stories. Each layer of these instructs us into some level of personal philosophical realization.

These layers of philosophy merge with each other, demonstrating to us that no school of thought can represent full reality. Each school projects a facet; all the facets together make up the still incomplete picture of truth.

The text tells us in picturesque detail about the states of our awareness and all its different rungs. It is not satisfied with talking about three states — wakefulness, dream and sleep — and the fourth, *turīya*. It speaks of all different permutations of these such as wakeful–wakeful, wakeful–dream, wakeful–sleep and so on, and then the state of a *yogī* in daily life wherein the fourth is interwoven with all the other ones.

YV speaks of these states at cosmic level; it tells stories and parables of cosmic wakefulness, cosmic dream, cosmic sleep and cosmic enlightenment.

It serves as a practical guide to enlightenment. It not only enlightens through philosophical discourses, it gives guidance into practical methods of contemplation, and of meditation, for those who would understand the methods and practise them.

It will grip you with its narratives and will take you to lofty skies of thought, imagination that methodically leads to illumination.

If one truly wishes to comprehend and absorb this mega-lyric of philosophy and an epic of the stories of enlightenment, then one needs to become fluent in Sanskrit; fluent, nothing less than that will do.

The second best access to *YV* is by reading the translations in Indian languages such as Hindi or Bangla or Tamil and so on. English is not the language for translating this mega-lyrical epic but I admire those who courageously undertake such a formidable task. There are some shortened versions and paraphrases of this beautiful text available also in English. I found the excerpts of *YV* translated by Christopher Chapple[1] to be specially lyrically evocative in English. In addition the translations of the shortened versions such as *Laghu-Yoga-Vāsiṣṭha* of Abhinanda are also very helpful. One may easily search and find these translations.

Our purpose here is not to give a complete summary of *Yoga-Vāsiṣṭha* but only to show the context of the place of *Bhagavad-Gītā* portion in the entire scheme of the lengthy spiritual–philosophical epic. The very scheme of the composition of *YV* is part of the Indian tradition of story telling in the form of stories within stories. Here is the brief schema.

The text begins by following the tradition of *maṅgalācaraṇa*, three invocation and prayer verses of homage to divinity:

The One from whom all beings shine forth (*appear*) *and*
(*in whom*) *they are stable* (*in continuity*),
Into whom they go into pacification (*dissolution*)
Unto That Truth-self (satya-ātman),
prostration (namaḥ).

From Whom (*proceed*) *knower, knowledge, knowable,*
the perceiver, the ground of perception and perceivable,
agent (*of action = doer*), *cause* (*and process of*) *act,*

---

1 His work is not yet published at the time of this writing but will soon see the light of publication.

unto That Cognition-self (jñapti-ātman),
prostration (namaḥ).

One from Whom flash forth sprays of bliss (ānanda)
in the sky and on earth,
(*Who is*) *the life*(*-force*) *of all,*
Unto That Brahman-*bliss-self* (brahma-ānanda-ātman)
prostration (namaḥ).

Then the story begins. The brāhmaṇa named Sutīkṣṇa has his mind filled with doubts, goes to the *āśrama* of sage Agasti and asks him the way to spiritual liberation (*mokṣa*). Agasti tells him:

As the birds fly with both wings in the sky
so does one attain the supreme state
by (*following*) *both knowledge* (jñāna) *and action* (karam).

In the context Agasti tells him the narrative of Agniveśya and his son Kāruṇya. The latter has studied all the Vedas and supporting texts (*veda-aṅgas*) and has returned to his home. Here he abandons all ritual and other acts, Agniveśya questions him about the abandonment. Kāruṇya tells him of the conflict he has between diverse scriptural statements, some impelling one to the sacramental acts and others saying that liberation is to be achieved only through renunciation. He does not know which teaching to take to his heart.

Here starts another narrative, that of King Ariṣṭanemi and the Sage Vālmīki.

An *apsaras*[2] named Suruci is sitting on a Himalayan mountain peak surrounded by her other *apsaras* friends. She sees overhead a *devadūta* (messenger of gods) passing by in the sky and, out of natural curiosity, she asks him where is he coming from and where is he going.

2 *Apsaras*, a species of celestial maidens who are epitome of sensuality, beauty, arts, dance and music. They are frequently reported in the Purāṇas and in Indian folk tales to descend to earth and also sport or otherwise interact with humans. Their male counterparts are *gandharvas*.

The *devadūta* tells her the story of a king who has renounced his throne in favour of his son and withdrawn for ascesis to the mountain Maddening Fragrance (Gandhamādana). His power of purification and ascesis comes to the notice of Indra, the king of gods, as it often does in numerous such stories. Indra has ordered the *devadūta* to take a *vimāna*[3] to the mountain on earth and invite the ascetic king to ascend in the *vimāna* and come to dwell in paradise.[4]

The *devadūta* follows the command and flies down to the ascetic king's mountain dwelling and there extends Indra's invitation to him. At this the king inquires into the nature of this paradise, what all are the flaws and positive points about paradise and what all transpires there.

Devadūta replies that with highest quality karmas one enters the highest paradise, with middling acts a middling one, and with lower quality the lower paradise. It is also explained that the residents of paradise are subject to the same kind of jealousies and such other attributes (as on earth).[5]

Upon this, as *devadūta* explains to the inquiring *apsaras*, the ascetic king refuses the invitation to enter such a paradise. He is only interested in the pursuit of *mokṣa*. He says:

I do not wish to enter a paradise that is such kind of fruition.
Henceforth, I shall undertake very severe ascesis;
Then I shall abandon this impure cadaver
Like a snake sheds its skin.

---

[3] Celestial flying vehicle of the *devas*. This particular one is well attended by the *apsaras*es, furnished with musical instruments and so on.

[4] Paradise in all Sanskrit, Pāli and Prākr̥t texts is not to be confused with final salvation or spiritual liberation (*mokṣa*). It is a world made of subtler matter, an abode of subtler and intense pleasures, and a time scale very different from that of the earthlings. Once one's good karma is exhausted, one reverts and re-incarnates into mortal existence.

[5] Compare the gods of the Greek myths.

O devadūta, *the way you came* (*riding*) *this* vimāna,
so go back the same way to the presence of great Indra.
Prostration be to you![6]

Upon this the *devadūta* returns to Indra and tells him what all the king has said in reply to his invitation. Indra recognizes that the king will not be tempted to a station lower than supreme liberation. Now that the king has passed this test, Indra commands *devadūta* in a very sweet voice to take the *vimāna* again, go back to the king and take him to Sage Vālmīki and there to petition the sage:

Great Sage, this king is endowed with humility and discipline.[7]
He is beyond worldly colouring and attractions[8] *and desires not heaven.*
Do, then, O Great Contemplative Sage (mahāmuni),
awaken in him the (*realization*) *of "Thatness"* (tattva),[9]
so that, suffering from the sorrows of the world(*liness*)
he will go to liberation (mokṣa).

Devadūta obeys the command, brings the king to the presence of Vālmīki and conveys Indra's petition to the sage. The sage welcomes the king very lovingly and inquires about his well-being (*kuśala*)[10]. The king replies:

Blessed One, knower of the thatness (tattva) *of* dharma,

---

6 This prostration is by way of bidding farewell and asking him to leave.

7 The word *vinīta* denotes both "humble" and "disciplined".

8 For the word *rāga*, see explanation in our Commentary on *Yoga-Sūtras of Patañjali* 1.12, 15-16; 2.3, 7-8; available from ahymsinpublishers@gmail.com

9 The word *tattva* literally means "thatness", that is, reality as it is, innate and inner nature of any aeons. The word is translated by other commentators in many different ways.

10 For more on this word, see our section on it in our *Philosophy of Hatha Yoga* available from ahymsinpublishers@gmail.com

highest among those who have known what ought to be known,[11]
That I have been blessed by seeing you,
that alone is my well-being.
I do wish to inquire, do teach me unobstructed,
How do I obtain release from the torment of the worldly sorrows?

Upon this the Sage Vālmīki offers:

Listen, King, I will narrate to you the complete Rāmāyaṇa.
Listening to this, and having absorbed [its teaching] with diligence
You will be liberated-while-living (jīvan-mukta).
I have seen (the purity of your) nature.
I will narrate to you the Dialogue of Vasiṣṭha and Rāma,
The beautiful story of the means to liberation.
Do listen, wise one.

Upon this the king inquires as to who this Rāma is and whether he is a bound soul or a liberated one. Vālmīki tells him that [even though Rāma is an ever-liberated one], he has come into temporary bondage due to four different curses (*śāpas*) placed on Viṣṇu (whose incarnation (*avatāra*) Rāma is) by different sages. For this reason, Rāma had to be reminded of his own transcendental nature as Self.[12]

Here we have given a summarized and paraphrased story of the sixty-six verses of the very first chapter. The next level of the narrative continues.

The second chapter (*sarga*) also begins with a *maṅgalācaraṇa* of one verse:

In the heaven, on earth, in the sky
outside and inside me
the all-pervasive one who shines

---

[11] On this see our *Commentary on Yoga-Sūtras* 2.27.

[12] Throughout this text, we use "self" to indicate individuated self (*jīvātman*) and Self for the transcendental One (*parama-ātman*).

as the very self of luminosity (avabhāsa-ātman)
— *unto Him the All-Self, Self of all* (sarva-ātman)
prostration (namaḥ).

On this verse the commentator Ānanda-Bodhendra Sarasvati (ABS) gives a very closely printed fifty-one-line commentary revealing great depths of philosophy.

As it is the ancient tradition to state who is a qualified person (*adhikārin*)[13] to be given any specific branch of knowledge, Vālmīki proceeds to state the *adhikārin* for this teaching.

I am bound; may I become liberated —
one who has this determination,
neither totally ignorant nor (fully) wise,
such a one has adhikāra *in this text and teaching* (śāstra).

Then Vālmīki proceeds to state the connection between the *Rāmāyaṇa* of the first part and this one of the second part.

When he had composed the first *Rāmāyaṇa*, he recited it to his beloved disciple Bharadvāja. At some forest venue on the Meru[14] mountain, Bharadvāja recited it to Brahmā (creator, one of the divine trinity who is also the one who reveals knowledge). Brahmā, pleased, offers Sage Bharadvāja to ask for a boon (*vara*). The latter asks:

O Blessed Lord, God of past and future,
The boon that interests me is:
Please teach me that whereby the common people (janatā)
may be freed of suffering.

Brahmā advises him to approach Vālmīki to compose such a text. Thereupon Brahmā himself accompanies Bharadvāja to Vālmīki's

13 On this word see our Commentary on the first *sūtra* of the *Yoga-Sūtras of Patañjali.*

14 Central mountain, the pivot of the earth. The same word is also used for the spine.

āśrama (spiritual sanctuary), makes the request personally to Vālmīki to compose a text that "would serve the world like a ship to have them cross the worldly ocean" and then, as is the wont of incarnations (*avatāra*s), *deva*s and *siddha*s (disembodied adepts), he simply makes a disappearance from right in front of their eyes, says Vālmīki, like a wave that had arisen in the ocean and vanished.

Vālmīki then asks Bharadvāja as to what was this all about and he is told of what had transpired between him and Brahmā. Thereupon Vālmīki, in order to obey the command of Brahmā, begins to compose and recite this second part of *Rāmāyaṇa* to Bharadvāja. He gives to Bharadvāja the names of sixteen grand personalities of *Rāmāyaṇa* including eight of his ministers[15] (*mantrin*s) who were all

sama-nīrāga-cetas	=	of a mind even and free of worldly colourings,
jīvan-mukta	=	living-liberated,
mahātman	=	great souls,
yathā-prāpta-anuvartin	=	following whatever comes their way,

thus (ABS) inwardly liberated and externally doing whatever actions and duties need to be performed.

The second chapter ends with this verse (here we follow ABS):

One who had fallen into the shoreless world-ocean
(but) whose highest strength in knowledge has been made firm,
having found the internal even-flow (sama-rasatva) *by determining the reality* (yukti),
neither falls into sorrow such as of separation from loved ones, nor goes into depression,

---

15 The tradition of a ministerial cabinet of eight is a very ancient one. See *Manu-Smṛti* 7.54 where it is stated that the king should appoint seven or eight ministers. This practice continued even up to the time of the Marāṭhās where it was called *aṣṭa-pradhāna*.

and has vanquished the root (of the two) namely the fever of ego, with a self that is in unexcelled bliss, remains ever satiated.

The narrative continues for the remaining 28,000+ verses.

As the main body of the story, Sage Vasiṣṭha enlightens Rāma. The thirty-three chapters of the first section (*sarga*) and two chapters of the second one, total of thirty-five chapters with 1,146 verses tell us the story of how the teaching of Vasiṣṭha began. We have already summarized the first two chapters of the first section. The story of Rāma begins in the third chapter.[16]

Rāma has not yet turned sixteen and he chooses to go on pilgrimages of all sacred spots in all four directions. Having visited the famous pilgrim centres and sacred rivers he returns home but soon lapses into a state of deep sadness. He takes interest in nothing that would excite or entice others. Day and night he is pondering over the suffering of the beings who are caught in the cycles of transmigration and the futility of worldly pursuits and interests.

In the meantime, the Sage Viśvāmitra arrives bearing the disturbing news of his *āśrama* being attacked by evil beings who desecrate his fire sacraments as he has the vows of completing the observance in ten days and is being troubled. He asks Daśaratha, Rāma's father, for the latter to accompany him to fight these disruptive forces. Daśaratha is scared for his young son who is barely sixteen years old yet, has not mastered many weapons, has no experience of battles. How could he protect the *āśrama*? The king offers to accompany the sage himself and give battle to those who disturb his sacrament. The sage becomes angered at this refusal. But the family's guru Sage Vasiṣṭha persuades the old king to summon Rāma to the court.

---

16 The well-known *Vālmīki Rāmāyaṇa* (*VR*) makes no suggestion of Rāma's sadness, inquiry into metaphysical knowledge or Vasiṣṭha's teachings in this regard. The story of *YV* seems to fit somewhere in *VR*. Bāla-Kāṇḍa *sarga*s 19-21.

The messenger proceeds to bring Rāma but shortly returns alone bringing the message of what seemed Rāma's very depressed state since his arrival back from the pilgrimage. They tell those present how Rāma just sits alone in deep thought and answers to nothing; does not eat; does not play; does not laugh, sing or cry. The messenger reports further that Rāma says "I am coming in a moment" but then does not stir.

Viśvāmitra discerns correctly:

> *Do bring Rāma here hurriedly. This confusion of Rāma is not from any crisis or attraction; it is a symptom of the awakening of one who has discrimination and dispassion.*
>
> *Let Rāma come and we shall remove his confusion in a moment like a wind blowing away a cloud from the mountaintop.*

A chain of messengers is sent to bring Rāma but in the meantime Rāma comes on his own, prostrates to his father, the sages and all the venerable elders. The father calls him over to sit in his lap and speaks to him lovingly and soothingly. Sages Vasiṣṭha and Viśvāmitra ask him the cause of his confusion. His reply begins in chapter 12 and goes on to the end of chapter 31 in 674 beautiful and forceful verses. It is an eloquent speech of deepest wisdom about the futility of worldly involvements. In itself it constitutes supreme teaching of metaphysical truths and dispassion towards worldly involvements.

After elaborating on his contemplative concerns, he requests the sages present to teach him the right way and method and emphatically sums up his determination (1.31.16-27):

> There is no possibility of diminishing (this sorrow) without proper way and method (*yukti*), so do tell me the best and sufficient method so that practising accordingly the sorrow no longer comes to me. Or, just tell me the method for right practice; how, wherewith, what, done with a high mind first, whereby the mind comes to restfulness and highest purification. Blessed one, (do

teach me) as you know for turning off my confusion; tell me of that by which definitely the noble ones (*sādhu*) indeed achieved sorrowlessness.

Or, if such a method, O *Brahman*-(knower), does not exist, or one clearly exists but no one tells me, and if I do not find that unexcelled restfulness by myself, in that case I will abandon all movement, go into a state of non-ego; I will not eat, I will not drink water, I will not wear clothing, nor will I indulge in any activities like bathing, giving, eating and so forth.[17] Nor do I stay in the activities whether in cordial conditions or in crisis. I (will) want absolutely nothing except to renounce my body, O Contemplative Sage; only free of all malice, devoid of "Meum" without any anxiety I (will) sit here absolutely silent as though painted in a picture. Abandoning in sequence the awareness of exhalation and inhalation I (will) abandon the calamitous inhabitation named "body".

> *Neither am I of this (body and world) nor is anyone else mine; I extinguish myself like an oilless lamp. Abandoning all, then I abandon this cadaver.*

Vālmīki said:

> *Rāma, charming and delightful like immaculate cooling moon, his mind blooming with the highest thoughts, having spoken thus, then, like a blue-throated peacock who makes his cry towards heavy clouds and then (ceases) as though wearied, fell silent.*

Upon hearing Rāma's eloquent speech, all the ladies of the palace, the courtiers, sages, all sit spellbound. The celestial sages, too have heard the adorable words. They shouted *sādhu*! *sādhu*! (well spoken! well spoken!). They sprinkled celestial blossoms on Rāma for full twelve minutes (fourth part of a *muhūrta* which is 48 minutes

---

[17] He is describing the daily schedule of a well brought up person in which first one cleans one body, then gives some charity, then eats.

in modern parlance), forming a veritable canopy over him. They spread the word throughout the heavens about this great council and all celestial sages such as Nārada, Vyāsa, Pulaha and others, all gathered, descended — whole army of them — and were duly honoured, full of poetic praises for Rāma.

Then Viśvāmitra said:

Rāma, there is nothing that is left to be known by you.
You are yourself highest among the knowing ones.
You have come to experiential knowledge (vijñāna) *by your own subtle intelligence.*
It only needs a little refinement.
Your wisdom is like that of Śuka the son of Vyāsa.

[*Comment*: Here ensues Rāma's question about Śuka and Viśvāmitra narrates the wisdom dialogue of Śuka and King Janaka.]

Viśvāmitra continues and advises that Vasiṣṭha the family guru carry out the teaching as his preceptor. Vasiṣṭha says:

> Venerable sage, as you command; I shall pass on the knowledge that Brahmā had conferred in the past on the Niṣadha mountain and I remember it in full and unfragmented.

It is here with the third chapter of section 2, that Vasiṣṭha's teaching really begins.

In one chapter close to the end of *YV* (6.II.213.1-50) Vasiṣṭha tells Rāma that in another life a similar dialogue had ensued between them when Rāma was the disciple and Vasiṣṭha was the guru.

> In some ancient aeon, there was the image of Consciousness consisting of (reality stated in texts) such as "Thou art *ātman* the self". The Consciousness-image had taken the form of guru and disciple in a forest [hermitage].

> There I had been the guru and you were then the disciple and you, (sitting) in front (as chief disciple), having an elevated and wise faculty of intelligence, asked me (the same question).

The disciple had asked the same question(s) and the guru had answered likewise but at that time the disciple did not grasp it, had to go through other-worldly existences and now the scenario is being repeated.

> Thus did you hear from me as a disciple in the past but did not awaken and comprehend (*buddhavān*). Thereupon, you were born in other existences. Today, born here, you are asking me the same very question.

This time Rāma has grasped it and become enlightened.

In chapter 214 the celestial beings rain down a shower of flowers and play celestial music in celebration of such a momentous event as Rāma's enlightenment. ABS expounds on verse 214.5:

> All were sitting in the council in their respective seats according to rank, such as
>
> *Vasiṣṭha at the highest and central seat,*
> *then the contemplative sages* (munis),
> *below them* (*king*) *Daśaratha, Rāma and others,*
> *then the ministers and knights,*
> *then the citizens.*
>
> They all gathered those celestial flowers and presented reverently their handfuls at Vasiṣṭha's feet and made salutations (*namaḥ*) to him as their odours of sweat etc. were cleansed with the coolness and fragrance of the celestial flowers, and they had (through the precepts) abandoned their sufferings of illness, hunger, thirst, fatigue as well as the sorrows [that arise] from birth and death and so forth.

Here, from among the listeners, the seniormost, Daśaratha, Rāma's father, utters most lyrical eight (6-13) verses in gratitude to the preceptor.

Rāma then speaks in words that are reminiscent of Arjuna's words in *MB-BhG* where he surrenders to Kr̥ṣṇa. In the verses below (our italics to indicate the phrases compared) we give references to the *MB-BhG* parallel verses or fragments thereof. Rāma says:

> *naṣṭo mohaḥ padaṁ prāptaṁ tvat-prasādān* munīśvara ।
> sampanno 'ham ahaṁ satyam atyantam avadāta-dhīḥ ॥
> — 14 = *MB-BhG* 18.73
>
> *sthito 'smi gata-sandehaḥ* sva-bhāve brahma-rūpiṇi ।
> nir-āvaraṇa-vijñānaḥ kariṣye vacanaṁ tava ॥
> — 15 = ibid
>
> *smṛtvā smṛtvā* 'mṛtāseka-saukhyadaṁ vacanaṁ tava ।
> *arhito 'pi ca śānto 'pi hṛṣyāmīva muhur muhuḥ* ॥
> — 16 = Cp. Sañjaya in *MB-BhG* 18.76
>
> *naiva me 'dya kṛtenārtho nākṛteneha kaścana* ।
> yathā sthito 'smi tiṣṭhāmi tathaiva *vigata-jvaraḥ* ॥
> — 17 = (Cp. Kṛṣṇa in *MB-BhG* 3.18, 30)

O Master among the contemplative sages (muni),
by your grace, confusion has vanished, pedestal has been achieved.
I am fulfilled. I am Truth (Brahman),
with exceedingly sharpened wisdom. — 14

I am stabilized, with doubts having gone,
in my innate nature (svabhāva) *that is* Brahman-*form.*
Knowledge through direct experience is unveiled.
I shall do as you have spoken (*to me*). — 15

Remembering over and over your words
that confer comfort of soaking in ambrosia,
whether I am honoured (*or dishonoured*), *I am at peace*
and yet, again and again, as if, I am rejoicing.[18] — 16

I have no purpose with the accomplished nor with unaccomplished.
I stay the same as I am in stability,
Freed of the fever(*ishness arising from*
whatever duty may be at hand). — 17

---

[18] "As if rejoicing" even though I am in a state of equanimity.

I have now seen the way (by your teaching);
What other kind of vision or view can there be?
O, the ground (of this restful state) is expansive.
O, how the people (without this knowledge) suffer! — 18

No foe have I nor friend, nor (inner and outer) field,[19] *nor anyone good or bad person.*
This universe (of consciousness), agitated, was difficult to understand,
(and now) the same one is pacific, beautiful in her limbs. — 19

How would someone know this without your compassion.
How can a child cross the sea without a bridge or a ship? — 20

I have seen the end of boundaries of prosperities (seeing ātman),
— of views and vision (having the vision of ātman),
— of sciences (having seen this transcendental science),
— of calamities (having seen the end of the universes),
— of (adorned) words (having heard the beautiful words here),
— of visible loci (having seen the locus of God). — 24

In the same context, Nārada, Viśvāmitra (two sages) and the brothers Lakṣmaṇa and Śatrughna, all, confer adulation upon the great preceptor for the teaching received.

In the final chapters (Nirvāṇa-Prakaraṇa Part II, chapters 215-16) Vālmīki winds up the story to Bharadvāja and tells him that thus Rāma's spiritual sadness was uplifted and Rāma and others, listening to Vasiṣṭha, rose above all sorrow.

> You, Bharadvāja, my son, are yourself a person of freed intelligence and today, listening to this text of liberation (*mokṣa-saṁhitā*) you have become even more free.
>
> These sacred (teachings of the) means and methods of liberation grant direct experience. Even a child listening to these (would)

---

[19] *Kṣetra* (field). We urge our readers to consult *BhG* chapter 13 to understand what is meant by a "field".

go to the knowledge of That (transcendental reality), leave alone someone like yourself.

Then, all those who have been mentioned in the first chapter wind up the different layers of the narrative. King Ariṣṭanemi, the *devadūta*, the *apsaras* on the mountaintop, Agniveśya, Kāruṇya, Agasti and Sutīkṣṇa: among these the seeker–listeners express their gratitude to their respective narrator–preceptors who grant all the blessings.

Sutīkṣṇa, with whose question the narrative began, closes the chapter and the text by expressing gratitude to his guru Agasti (here with ABS aid):

Nescience and its effects have now vanished.
I have received the unexcelled knowledge.
The way all acts are performed in the light of lamp,
So it is in the Witness,[20] *with flashing illumination.*

In whom all secular and sacramental acts are performed with the mind preceded by spontaneous vibration (spanda[21]),
the way bracelet, armband, bangle[22] *and anklet are only forms of gold,*
as the arrays of waves are in the water,

so, the one from whom this entire ground of perceptibles (arises) —
That alone is this entire universe.
Full, complete, perfect is established in the full, complete, perfect.[23]

---

20 The transcendent remains a neutral witness unaffected and unaltered by the events of the universe.

21 Here we encourage the reader to study the philosophy of vibration (*spanda*) as taught in Kāśmīr Śaivism.

22 The dictionaries like that of Monier-Williams and Apte translate both *aṅgada* and *keyūra* as meaning an upper armband.

23 All three words are translations of the single word *pūrṇa*, the full dwelling in the full.

I, therefore, follow (the duties) as they arise.
Who can transgress the words of the saintly noble.
Blessed One, by your grace I am now sustained,
having come to know what ought to be known.[24]

Gratified and fulfilled am I.
I fall on the ground in prostration like a staff.[25]
By what act can one cease to be indebted to the guru?
Therefore, the disciples' self-surrender with body, speech and mind —
Only through that may one obtain the uplifting from debt; not by any other act.
Master, by your grace am I brought across the ocean of worldly being
so the entire network of the universe is (now) filled with Full Bliss.
That "Who" becomes revealed by listening to the sāman[26]
sarvaṁ khalv idam brahma taj-jalān iti
— *Chāndogya Upaniṣad* 3.14.1

All this is Brahman *from whom all is born and into whom dissolves*
Unto That Brahman-*self* (brahma-ātman) *prostration* (namaḥ).

The text itself closes with a homage to sage Vasiṣṭha (6.II.156.26) in words identical to a verse we often sing to the guru, the concluding verse of *Guru-Gītā*.

---

24 For this concept of *jñāta–jñeya* see *sūtra* 2.27 in our *Commentary on the Yoga-Sūtras of Patañjali.*

25 *Daṇḍavat praṇāma* is still performed to one's elders where one lies on the ground touching the elders feet with stretched out hands, eight limbs touching the ground. This is what is meant when the English word "prostration" is used.

26 A passage from the Upaniṣad of the *Sāmaveda*, namely, *Chāndogya Upaniṣad.*

brahmānandaṁ	:	to (the embodiment of) the very bliss that is *Brahman*
parama-sukha-daṁ	:	to one who grants ultimate comfort and pleasure
kevalaṁ	:	to the Solo One[27]
jñāna-mūrtiṁ	:	to one who is the image of knowledge and wisdom
dvandva-atītaṁ	:	to one who is beyond dualities and pairs of opposites
gagana-sadr̥śaṁ	:	to one who is similar to space (clear and unalterable)
"tat tvam asi"-ādi-gamyam	:	to the one attainable through great sentences such as "thou art that" (*Chāndogya Upaniṣad* 6.8.7 et seq.)
ekaṁ	:	to the One
nityaṁ	:	to the perennial one
vi-malaṁ	:	to immaculate one
acalaṁ	:	to motionless, immovable one
sarva-dhī-sākṣi-bhūtaṁ	:	to one who is the witness to all (processes taking place) in the faculty of discrimination–intelligence–wisdom (*dhī*) of all
bhāvātītaṁ	:	to one who has transcended (modifications and modulations of) "becomings" (arising out of Being)
tri-guṇa-rahitaṁ	:	to one devoid of three *guṇa*s (of *prakr̥ti*)[28] — to such a one, Vasiṣṭha, we humbly prostrate.

The only difference between the *Guru-Gītā* and *YV* versions is in the last half of the fourth quarter as follows:

---

27 This suggests the state of *kaivalya* as taught in the *Yoga-Sūtras*.

28 For the three *guṇa*s, see *BhG* chapters 14, 17 and 18.

Guru-Gītā: sad-guruṁ taṁ namāmi	:	*I prostrate to that noble* guru.
YV: śrī-vasiṣṭhaṁ natāḥ smaḥ	:	*We humbly prostrate to Śrī Vasiṣṭha.*

As the concluding verses of *YV* and of *Guru-Gītā* are nearly identical, it will be difficult to determine as to which text is the original and which one is a modified borrowing as the dates of both texts cannot be ascertained. Our sense is that *YV* version is the older one or both are borrowings from a common stock of wisdom.

One amazing point about this text. Rāma has been called to his father Daśaratha's court where he expresses his sadness in *vairāgya*. Thereupon the teaching ensues.

The narrative of Vālmīki to Bharadvāja is divided into irregular lengths of days (*divasa*s), totalling eighteen. The verse indicating a break however occurs only fourteen times. The indication of the *divasa* ending is given also thirteen times. But, with some of the numbers missing (7, 9, 14, 15), the other number of *divasa*s are indicated.

The verse reads:

vālmīkir uvāca:
ity uktavaty atha munau divaso jagāma,
sāyantanāya vidhaye 'stamino jagāma ।
snātuṁ sabhā kṛta-namas-karaṇā jagāma,
śyāmākṣaye ravi-karaiś ca sahājagāma ॥

Vālmīki said:

When the Sage had thus spoken the day ended.
The king[29] (*sun*) *went to set, to perform the evening rituals.*
The council, having offered prostrations, went to bathe.
At the vanishing of the night (*the council*) *returned with the sun.*

The end of eighteenth *divasa* is marked at 6.I.86.29 and the

[29] Double entendre here. The king is the sun that just set and the human king went to perform the evening rituals.

seventeenth is marked at 6.II.95.31. These discrepancies cannot be reconciled and may be attributed to scribes' errors.

Here, another thought occurs. The recitation of sacred texts to oneself (*pāṭha*) or to an audience (*kathā*) is a tradition still very widely practised among hundreds of millions of the devout in India. The texts, like the *Rāmāyaṇa* and *Bhāgavata Purāṇa* are recited with formal division of portions to be read/recited in a given day. It is possible that some devotee somewhere also started a similar tradition with *Yoga-Vāsiṣṭha* but it lapsed and the formal division of *divasa*s of *YV* recitation got corrupted at the hand of the scribes not familiar with this oral tradition, unlike the texts like *Rāma-carita-mānasa*, the Awadhi language version by Tulsīdās, which is the most popular version of *Rāmāyaṇa* in north India. The same may be the case with the *kathā* recitations of the versions in other languages like Bangla, Odiya, Nepali and so forth. Hanneder (2006: 132ff) refers to a number of such readings done for the benefit of historical figures. However, there is no evidence existent for our conjecture that there may have been a formal division of *divasa*s as in these recitals.

The mention of Rāma and Vasiṣṭha, together with other members of the assembled council taking breaks, occurs at 3.4.1-34, 5.1-3 and 6.I.1.

Hanneder (2006: 23) also mentions a similar break at 6.I.69 perhaps this reference is to the Kashmir version of *Mokṣopāya*.

Is it possible that the entire dialogue and the profound spiritual experiences woven in-between, all, occurred in only these few sittings? To a believing *sādhaka* (aspirant practitioner) who has been given the disciplines leading to a lengthy duration of sitting steady (*āsana-siddhi*) is still amazing but it is possible between the master and disciples of a very high calibre who are close to enlightenment.

To an average reader and a neutral scholar all the discrepancies suggest that the composition of this text may be the work of years of inspired labour and/or a collation of texts that have been interpolated and integrated from time to time. We await the discovery of the *ur*-text by the modern scientific scholars.

The stories in *YV* are illustrative of the philosophy and their purpose is to expand our consciousness beyond the limitations of our present personal space-times. Here we cannot give the complete stories but only brief excerpts taken out of their context. We present a few excerpts and paraphrases from the vast text to illustrate the contents of this philosophical mega-lyric. For example:

(1)

Once upon a time there was a king who had three sons. They all decided that the greatest thing they could do with their life-time would be to see the end of the universe. So they started out. They have been journeying now for the past 17,00,000 years and have not returned yet. — *YV* 6.II.131

(2)

In a city called Empty (*śūnya*) once there were three brothers. Two of whom were not born yet and the third one had not yet been conceived.

They conferred and decided to travel out, explore and have adventures. So they walked out together.

In their journey they rested under three trees, ate the fruits thereof and adorned themselves with the blossoms of the trees. Two of the trees had not yet grown and the third one was not yet planted.

In the midday heat they came upon three rivers. Two of which had no water then and one had never had any. The brothers frolicked in the rivers for a long time, drank water and refreshed themselves.

[They crossed the rivers in three boats two of which had no bottom and the third one was not yet built.[30]]

30 Text shown in square brackets is our addition.

After a long journey, they arrived in a city named "New Construction in Future" and settled in three houses, one of which had no walls and two were not built yet.

They cooked 99 kg[31] of food in three vessels, two of which had become like skulls and one had become as powder.

They invited three holy priests (brāhmaṇas) to dinner, two of whom had no body and the third one had no mouth.

Having fed the priests they gorged themselves, too and have lived in that Future City ever since.

[*Comment*: So it is with our fears, anxieties and desires]

— *YV* 3.101.1-39

(3)

Once there was a great sage living in a forest hermitage, committed to his askesis (*tapas*) and its practices. Now an *āśrama* is a place where the beings of opposite characters, like lion and deer, should roam free of fear and violence. A hunter terrified them and disturbed the peace of the *āśrama*. He would not listen to the sage to desist.

Finally, one day, the exasperated sage said to him: You have been infesting this *āśrama* far too long. Alright, infest then; be a mosquito!

The curse was effective and the hunter became a mosquito in the forest. The mosquito died. As the hunter's mind had been on the deer, and he had been terrifying the deer all his life, he was born a deer now to feel the terror himself.

That karma worked off, he was born again as a man. The part of the cruel karma now washed off, there arose in him a desire to pursue sacred knowledge. Accordingly he approached the sage who told him: You need to go through much purification. Abide with me and do *tapasyā* (ascetic spiritual practices).

31 An ancient measure, *droṇa*.

Gradually, knowledge began to dawn on him. He had many questions. There arose in him the desire to know:

> There is *bhava-jagat* and there is *saṅkalpa-jagat*. One is the empirical world of times and spaces as we know them and the other is the world of pure intention, will, creation through imagination or visualization. How do the two synchronize? Where do they meet?

Upon being asked this question, the sage narrated as follows:

> In my younger days, when I led a worldly life but had gained some powers and insights, one day I was sitting by the side of a friend who was asleep. He seemed to be dreaming. I wondered what he might be dreaming about. So I gathered my consciousness into a pinpoint and entered into his dream.
>
> He was in a beautiful world. I loved that world. I wandered about and explored it. I met a beautiful lady and married her, established a business. Acquired land and property, and had lovely children. All that made me very happy. Decades passed.
>
> But, there was always a nagging doubt. Somewhere in me the consciousness said that somehow I am not of this world. Who am I? Where have I come from? What is my purpose in life?
>
> The doubts and questions continued to arise but I also continued with my marital and business duties. However, when the children were older, I wandered off again, this time in search of a wise man who would answer my questions. A hundred years had passed.
>
> In a forest clearing I found an *āśrama* where a great sage sat. I prostrated to him and presented my queries.
>
> He looked at me and said sharply: You are not of this dream world. You are from the world of wakefulness. GO!
>
> I recollected my reality, gathered my consciousness into a pinpoint of light and emerged into the wakeful world.

I sat by the side of my friend who was dreaming.

A hundred years?

Only a micro-moment had passed since I entered his dream.

(4)

Narrative of Līlā

> The story in fifty-two chapters (3.15-68) is an entire epic in its own right, with wars, battles and deaths and *nirvāṇa* of the leading figures, all in different worlds, in different spaces, with different time scales in each alternative space and yet interacting from one to the other.

Once upon a time, in a certain country there was a king named Padma. His queen's name was Līlā. The two were two bodies and one heart. Especially Līlā could not imagine ever being without her husband. So one day she asked a wise priest: Is there some way that one can prevent death so that my husband will never die and leave me alone?

The priest replied that there was no way one could live forever or could delay death and that death was inevitable.

The queen, unable to bear the thought of ever being separated from her beloved husband, undertook great concentrated practice of the worship of Sarasvatī (the Divine Mother of knowledge and wisdom).

After much *tapasyā*, Goddess Sarasvatī appeared to Līlā and offered her a boon. Līlā asked if it was possible to grant her husband immortality. Sarasvatī categorically said that was not possible but: "I promise that when he dies his soul will remain in this room. You should keep the body preserved till the day the soul returns. Furthermore, I grant that whenever you wish to see me, just remember me and I will appear before you".

In time the king died. Queen Līlā was distraught. She remembered to call Sarasvatī who appeared.

Līlā asked: Where is my husband now?

Right in this room but in another creation; a creation subtler, finer than this one, that is inside our present creation.

There is a world within a world within a world within a world, and this goes on from the infinitesimal to the infinite, from the infinite to the infinitesimal.

[*Comment*: Can you think of beings in an atom? Can you think of some beings for whom the solar system is an atom? So one creation is empty for the people, the beings of another creation. But it is possible for someone to attain the *siddhi*[32] that he can see the behaviour and the way of a finer or a grosser creation.]

Līlā now was very anxious to see her husband. Sarasvatī taught her the way of attaining that *siddhi*, so she could enter the finer creations. Thereupon Sarasvatī and Līlā, the goddess and the queen together, entered the creation where Līlā's husband was present. He was at that time, according to his *vāsanā*s (propensity from karmic thought processes), his *saṁskāra*s (subtle body imprints), experiencing the ripening fruition of his acts, his karmas, which can be experienced only in that creation.

They see him to be a sixteen-year-old king.

He had died here only a few moments ago, but now in the other creation they see him as sixteen-year-old prince on a throne.

Līlā was amazed. "How can sixteen years have passed that he was born here and he just died recently? Where is this creation, where is this kingdom now?"

Sarasvatī replied, "It is right in this room."

"All this empire?"

---

[32] Accomplishment of what to others appears to be a supra-material power.

"Yes." — Said the deity. In each miniscule atom of time and space there are uncountable other times and spaces. And the event that takes one moment in one world takes an aeon in another world.

[*Comment*: Just as a man lying right there on his bed in dream experiences years, so it is with all the worlds.]

The deity said, "You are amazed only at this one transition? Just about a week ago, your husband Padma was a brāhmaṇa and you were his wife of a brāhmaṇa caste."

"How can that be? I was queen and he was king."

"That was in that creation, now you are here. You don't trust me, don't believe me?"

So they took a step into another empire, from that into another, finer, creation. They see that the brāhmaṇa is dead. The small cottage where the brāhmaṇa used to live is now bereft of him. His sons, daughters, daughters-in-law are all wailing and lamenting.

Thus the deity (Sarasvatī) has taken Līlā a little step further back to show that she is now the wife of the brāhmaṇa.

One day the brāhmaṇa Vasiṣṭha is walking in the city with wife and sees the king's procession, with beautifully adorned elephant, marching bands and everything, passing in the city. In the brāhmaṇa's mind arose the desire, "I wish I were a king! Oh, it's so wonderful to be a king. Here I am living in a small hut, and — look at him!"

That desire established its seeds and developed its roots. These became his *saṁskāra*.

The wife of this brāhmaṇa, Arundhatī, was absolutedly devoted to her husband the brāhmaṇa Vasiṣṭha. So she undertook a long period of worship of the Goddess Sarasvatī. And Goddess Sarasvatī appeared to her and asked,

"What do you wish for?"

"I want that my husband should never die."

The goddess said, "That is not possible."

"Well, in that case, can you make it so that when my husband dies, his soul remains in this very room?"

So when the brāhmaṇa died, his wife was naturally forlorn, and in that grief she immolated herself with the body of the husband.

Sarasvatī continues — "This brāhmaṇa, because of the force of the intense desire that had arisen upon seeing the king's procession, was born as the King Padma in our creation-1, and you, because of your attachment, are born as his wife, the queen. And, because of the same *saṁskāra*, you did the same worship and expressed the same wish. You asked me to grant the same boon that you got there and now you have got here."

At this point Līlā wants to know, "What and what have I been?"

Now from this brāhmaṇahood they return to creation-2, where the sixteen-year-old king named Vidūratha is reigning. When they return they see the king is seventy years old. And the name of his wife is Līlā. . . . The story continues.

[*Comment*: The *YV* text actually goes into great detail about how she remembers herself, having been this or this or that and someone else. We have not completed this summary of Līlā story for lack of space here.[33]]

(5)

Once upon a time when I was the pure sky of consciousness, in that sky of consciousness arose the moonlight of awareness. I was then *Brahman*. I, *Brahman*, meditated upon my own being, my own nature, with the cool moonlight of awareness in the sky of consciousness that I was. During one of these meditations upon

[33] For an analysis and annotated Italian translation of Līlā's story, *vide* Bruno Lo Turco: Il Mokshopaya; lo spazio della consceincza come principio assoluto. Dodici Capitoli dal Lilopakhyana. Edizione critica e tradzione annotate. PhD Thesis, University of Roma, Rome 1998.

my own pure, sky-like, formless being, I noticed a tiny sprout of will called the will to creation. Just as a seed, planted in a flowerpot placed in the courtyard, begins to sprout when the rains fall, so the rain of my attention, my concentration, fell upon the seed of the will to create, and that seed began to sprout. Just as when, in deep sleep, the attention suddenly falls upon the seeds of creativity, and there sprouts a dream (and when the attention is withdrawn, the dream is folded back again and the person returns from sleep into wakefulness), so I see this universe unfolding as a dream within me who am the sky of consciousness.

As this rain of attention, volition, fell on the will to create, I saw within myself Earth, so with my attention I permeated this Earth, and I became the islands, the mountains, the grass, the trees. I became the minerals, the jewels, the gold and shining silver. Oh so many forests and trees, branches and twigs became my hairs; my body was filled with jewels; my body was ornamented with cities and villages and other habitations. I, having assumed the form of Earth, was filled with rivers, forests, seas, directions — east, west, north, south. I became the one on whom so many creatures roamed. The lilies bloomed on my body; the vines and creepers grew on me; the rivers and lakes were in the hair-roots of me — all of this network, consisting of duality, is in fact tranquil, non-dual.

On this earth I paid attention to the waters, and thereby through that attention in the sky of consciousness I also became waters — clear like sapphire. Then I, in my body of waters, rose and became clouds and gamboled in love-play with my wife, the lightning, becoming the taste of all things in the universe. I became so diversified that in trillions of creatures I became the essence of millions of their taste buds. Such pleasure of being water was mine, but I do not believe even that to be the experience of taste buds, but just this pure Self assuming that particular form. With my water body I have taken rides on the chariot of winds, and in the clear lanes of the sky I have roamed like fragrance. Though I am the pure conscious being, in order to see what the experience of being water is, within my own consciousness, I reduced the degree of my totality of consciousness and experienced the consciousness only of being water.

I became fires — an illumination, a light, a brilliance: I became the brilliance of the moon; I became the splendour that is in the sun; I became the light that is in the stars; I became the warmth that is in the fires. Because illumination consists predominantly of the quality of *sattva*, the visibility of all things, therefore, was my limbs. I became the father, giving birth to the white, blue and rosy colours — all of them that sleep in the lap of their father, the light. With my illumination I became the mirror for my brides, the parts of the sky, the directions.

I became the power of the winds to remove the mists of the night. I was the life essence of the moon, the sun and the fires. I became the colour in gold, in the emerald, in the ruby. With that power of illumination I became valour in man, and in the rainy season I became the lightning. With my power of brilliance I became God Indra's weapon to split apart the heads of the demons of darkness, and I became the courage in the heart of the lion. I became the fearlessness in the limbs of the warrior in the battlefield, the courage that can break through the strongest armour. Besides all this, I was also in my form as the sun, and I spread out my hands as rays and grabbed the mountaintops on the earths of all the universes. Within that illumination-form of mine, this whole Earth, to me, looked like a tiny village seen from a very high mountaintop.

When I took the form of the moon (as I was the illumination of the moon), I became a lake filled with *amṛta* (the ambrosia of immortality). I was the face of the beautiful lady called the Heavenly World. When I scattered myself on Earth in the form of the moonlight I was like the laughter of the lady called Night. And I was a little candle, too, for all the human beings walking around at night. In the form of fire I became a conflagration and burned forest upon forest. I created sounds that frightened many creatures who scampered in the shade of those trees. But then I was also the ritual fire who gathered sacrifices made by the people, and as such I turned those sacrifices into finer essences and passed them on to the gods of the subtler worlds. Sometimes I was in a blacksmith's shop changing the forms of iron into hammers; sometimes I was a mere spark. All of this I have been, my disciple.

With my attention passed on to that will of creativity, I became the winds. I made all the vines, creepers and leaves dance. I gathered the fragrances of lilies, roses and other flowers, and scattered them to the wide world; I came into the parks full of freshness and carried their freshness to the cities; I slept on the bed of clouds; I dried the sweat of the tired human beings; I was the fragrance of the flower called the sky. I was, as it were, a twin brother to the sounds that arise in space. I became the source of vitality moving and flowing in the limbs of all living beings, carrying fluids in their arteries; I was the thief plundering the jewels called the fragrances hidden deep inside the flowers. I had the power to pick up the mountains from their roots and scatter them. Such a powerful wind, too, I became! I turned water into ice, dried the mud, carried the clouds, moved the blades of grass, wafted fragrances from here to there and reduced the heat in the bodies of those who suffered.

In this form of earth, water, fire, I have lived in the bodies of trees, and in the form of trees I have sent down roots to suck the subtlest juices of food and moisture lying deep in the earth, and I have tasted them. I have tasted the way the tree tastes that moisture deep in the earth. I have lain about on the arctic snow. I have sung along with the cranes in the lotus forests. Through my will the suns and stars, taking all kinds of colours, have dwelt in my body. In my awareness of being the entire space of consciousness, I have gathered and worn the seven worlds as that many bangles around my wrists. When I was this whole universe, the very deepest parts of the earth were as the soles of my feet, and the top of this earth was, as it were, my belly, and the blue sky of Earth was my forehead. And yet, in all of these manifold forms, as I dwelt as the earth, as the water, as the fire, as the space, as the illumination, as the entire universe, I have never for one moment abandoned my true nature, my being pure consciousness.

I have taken all of these forms just as the pure power of consciousness alone creates all the cities in the dream. Yet the power of consciousness is not lost, and that dream and those dream cities are merely a mode, merely a note in the music of consciousness that has not thereby abandoned its nature of being music. So all of this *māyā* I have created, I have become. But I have not changed thereby.[34]

(6)

Narrative of Chūḍālā[35]

The story below is a summary of 3,288 verses of philosophy, propounded in twenty-four chapters (6.II.77-110), titled the *Narrative of Chūḍālā*.

Once upon a time there was a king named Śikhidhvaja. (From here on we shall call him the king.) He married a beautiful woman named Chūḍālā who was more accomplished in wisdom than him. After they had enjoyed their youthful passions and desires with each other for a long time, they realized that:

Youth passes like water dripping little by little
from a pot that has a tiny hole.
It disappears like waves that rise mighty and then vanish.
Death comes as certain as the fall of a ripe fruit.
Only the craving grows like a vine after the rainy season,
while the youth is on just for a while
like a mountain river that comes into flow
only during the monsoons.
Life is unreal like a magic show.

---

34 Previously published in this author's book *God* (pp. 67-72), available from ahymsinpublishers@gmail.com

35 Previously published in *Dawn Magazine*, Summer 1975. The magazine ceased publication soon after.

Let us look for something lasting, permanent, real.
Let us go after knowledge of the true Self.

Thereafter they paid their attention entirely to the medicine of the disease called the worldly cycles. Knowing that this plague that catches all has only one remedy — self-knowledge — they talked only of this matter between themselves.

The verses thus continue, but we shall try to make the long story short. The king was anguished and felt that she had gone somewhat insane and all the queen's efforts to bring realization to him failed. While she experienced the natural awakening of the *kuṇḍalinī*, the king went on as it were, measuring empty space by fistfuls. While she gave up all claims, out of naturally awakened wisdom, to being or non-being, to this or that, her husband made much endeavour to find the truth, but failed. With her realization, her powers grew. While in her husband's arms, she would also wander suddenly to hills and mountains and return like lightning even before he could realize that she was gone, but the king always thought of her as "my little woman, my ignorant housewife, O so lovable". She, too, refrained from exhibiting her powers to her husband who was yet unqualified, for he could not dream of receiving knowledge from his own "little wife".

The king undertook many acts of asceticism and austerity, practised meditation in lonely places, gave much charity, tried many fasts, looking for a remedy for this disease called the worldly cycle. Finally he declared his intentions to his wife to abandon his royal duties to go into a forest and live as a hermit. He said he now loved the forest environment as much as he had once loved her; for the way the mind can be turned off in the solitude of the forest is like no other place.

The queen tried to argue with him and said it was not yet time to leave his administrative duties; that he should not become responsible for creating anarchy in his kingdom by leaving the nation uncared for.

Especially Chūḍālā's discrimination grew, day by day, and she found that neither the body nor the senses nor the mind nor ego could be the True Self, but that the True Self is the Pure Consciousness Principle. Then suddenly enlightenment came to her and she declared:

All these; the Mind, Intellect and Senses,
All the plays of Consciousness
Unreal by themselves, as if a second moon,
a mere reflection
Only the great Consciousness is the great Existence
Oh how long it has been since I knew this
and have discovered this again!
There is neither this nor I, nor anything else, separate;
All is tranquil, one and Supreme.

So she lived in peace in the state of indescribable joy, but the king, who was yet far from the goal they had chosen together, could not understand what she was so happy about. While her beauty grew, his anxiety knew no end, and he questioned her:

As if regaining your youth again in this old age,
As if you have drunk the essence of the drink of immortality,
Growing more and more beautiful and glorious daily,
My dear one, what is it you have found?
Your mind has become so even, yet vigorous,
Tranquil and without craving,
Counting the three worlds like a blade of straw;
As if an impenetrable ocean of milk,
Your mind is filled with some strange bliss.
Though your limbs are exactly the same, tender and small,
Yet somehow you have grown.
Have you truly found amr̥ta *or something else*
That is even greater than the three worlds?

And she replied:

Neither something nor nothing have I abandoned

As I stand here before you.
And thus have I gained this glory.
By giving up all, I have found it All,
Thus do I stand in glory.
Now I know the truth of that something which is nothing
Thus do I stand in glory.
Contented with enjoyments unenjoyed,

Neither pleased nor anguished,
Thus do I stand in glory.
Alone in the inner space, in the absolute heart
I rejoice; I no longer delight in royal games,
Thus do I stand in glory,
I am this, I am not all this; I am real and I really am not.
I am All and I am nothing.

Thus do I stand in glory. . . .

"When the time is ripe, we will go together", she said. But he said, "Oh, no, we could not go together. Those forests and hermitages are not for women. Now, you listen to me and obey me", he said. "Just stay here and take care of the kingdom after I am gone."

She could not agree, so in the middle of the night, he told her he was leaving for *vīra-yātrā*. It was a custom that the king would often wander *in cognito* in his kingdom to inspect the efficiency of the administration in providing law and order and to render any help, unrecognized, to any citizen in need. But he actually went to live as a hermit. He went on making pilgrimages and again practising many austerities, but to no avail.

Meanwhile the queen had announced to the ministers that the king had left on a secret journey, leaving her in authority. From then on she carried on the work of the kingdom, and through her yogic power she also discovered the royal hermit's hideout. Using only her subtle body, she travelled to the king's abode, and remaining unseen, saw that there was still no peace in the king's mind. Self-realization was still far away from him, and so out of compassion, she decided to help him to attain the Highest Enlightenment.

Now, one of the first rules for a guru is to avoid whatever a would-be disciple would resist. Queen Chūḍālā knew that he would not receive knowledge from her, a "mere wife", so she took the form of a youthful sage, the son of a *ṛṣi*. For a great *yogī* there is no problem changing into such forms. The king saw this young man coming to his cottage and welcomed him. The acquaintance became a friendship, and the two became regular companions. The youth was named Kumbhaja.

The queen was at the same time running the kingdom in her Chūḍālā form, and was also visiting the king for metaphysical discussions in the form of this youth. The discussions gradually began to open the king's mental eye and he asked to be taken into the youthful sage's discipleship.

Chūḍālā, in her alter ego, continued to instruct him until the king finally realized that though he had given up his kingdom, his country and his wife, yet he had abandoned nothing, because there was now in his mind the thought of my forest, my hermitage, my renunciation. He burned his hermitage to the ground and yet Kumbhaja was not satisfied. Kumbhaja said that burning the hermitage, too, was an act of attachment. Gradually, the king was free of this attachment and false renunciation. He learned that just cutting the branches and twigs of the mind would not suffice. He learned to cut the very root of the mind through the meditation process and learned that the entire universe was his own meditation. He declared:

Oh, the view of the divisions of the worldly objects
The multitude of acts, incalculable of space, time, and sequence.
It has taken me so long to pacify it all.
But now I remain in the tranquil Brahman, *the Immutable Self.*
I go to peace. I blow out. I become still.
I go nowhere. I neither rise nor sit. I stand still,

The Self resting in the Self, benevolent, beautiful.
I am a purifying Silence.

Now it was time for him to be tested: The young handsome sage Kumbhaja, who was Chūḍālā herself, came to the king one day with a troubled expression. The king asked, "Why are you, a self-realized being, in a state of suffering?" Kumbhaja said that he was almost ashamed to tell him, but had no alternative.

As I was coming from the celestial world to see you, I saw the celestial sage Durvāsas who is known for his quick and sharp anger. Durvāsas was dressed in some very strange clothing and seeing him I couldn't help but laugh, and I said, "Durvāsas, excuse me but you are dressed like a woman". Durvāsas got very angry and immediately placed a curse on me, and said, "I, a woman! Well, from now on it will be you who will become a woman every night, while remaining a man in the day". I don't even want to go back to my celestial home, so embarrassed am I.

The king said:

> So what? The man and the woman are not of the true Self, the true Self is neither masculine nor feminine. What happens to the male and female bodies is of no concern to the inner life force. If you do not wish to go back to your heavenly world until this curse has passed, you may stay with me.

From then on Kumbhaja lived with the king, remaining a man in the day, and at the same time, serving as the queen in the kingdom, and sleeping in the same bed with the king in a female form, named Madanikā, at night. The king, who was above maleness and femaleness, was not concerned with the fact that he was sharing his bed with a woman.

It was time for further testing: Kumbhaja in his lady form, Madanikā, one night approached the king and said:

> I am a healthy woman, I have been living here with you for so long, and I have such strong passionate urges that a woman has

> for a man. We have been companions and friends and there is no greater joy in the world than to have a male–female companionship between two persons of like mind. I will not rest in peace unless you and I have a happy wedlock.

The king replied,

> So far as I am concerned, it makes not the slightest difference to me, for I am the Pure Self. If I live with a woman or marry her and satisfy her desires, it would be only for her satisfaction, while my Pure Self is completely untouched. For your happiness I shall marry you.

And so one full moonlit night they married, and in the day the royal hermit had the company of a handsome young man and at night he had a wife, and yet, while doing everything possible to keep Madanikā happy, he remained completely untouched in his spiritual being.

While his body and senses did their natural duties, the Pure Self remained tranquil.

Now Chūḍālā created from her yogic powers the figure of Indra, king of paradise, and this Indra and the other celestial deities appeared before the king, praising his knowledge and spirituality. He said that the king should now leave this world of ordinary mortals and come enjoy the pleasures of paradise, but the king said,

> What other paradise is there than what is in the Self? The contentment of the Spirit is a greater paradise than any and I have no desire for any other celestial pleasure.

Indra went his way, and the hermit's life continued until something further developed. One evening while the king was gone for meditation on the banks of the river, Chūḍālā created a very handsome youth. The king returned after dark and saw her (Madanikā) in the arms of this handsome youth, lost to the world! The king quietly turned away so as not to disturb their happiness. For him it was a matter of no concern whatsoever. But as Madanikā realized that the king was there, she freed herself and fell at her husband's feet and apologized profusely. But the king told her that it is natural for human beings to develop affection.

So whatever she had done could not surprise him. He could no longer be her husband, but she was welcome to share his cottage with her new-found husband. He thereafter treated Kumbhaja–Mandanikā with the same friendship as before and promised a home to Madanikā's new husband as well. It was then that Mandanikā suddenly appeared in her natural form as Chūḍālā. The king's enlightenment was now complete. Thereafter they rulled the kingdom together, following the *dharma* of the kṣatriya caste.

Chūḍālā declared:

I have no desire for enjoyment, nor for powers,
I live in Self-nature, accepting whatever comes.
Neither actions, nor this kingdom, nor even paradise
Lead me to any pleasure.
I remain without any agitation, whatever may happen.
This is pleasant, this unpleasant —
Such dichotomy has now vanished.
All is even to me as I dwell in tranquillity.

The king agreed:

Rightly have you stated this, Chūḍālā.
Keeping or renouncing a kingdom are just the same to me.
So free of thoughts of pleasant or unpleasant,
We shall dwell together in Self-nature, doing what is now at hand.

***

For some summaries of the stories in *YV*, see numerous publications of B.L. Atreya from 1934 onwards. For yet shorter summaries see Hanneder (2006).

***

The authorship of the text under discussion is attributed to sage Vālmīki.

The modern scholars like Hanneder, Slaje and Lo Turco, supporting much earlier view propounded by Divanji (1938), have shown that there are two recensions of the text:

1. an earlier shorter version titled *Mokṣopāya*, written in the Śāradā script of Kashmir was mainly transmitted in Kashmir, on which Bhāskarakaṇṭha's partial commentary is now in the process of being published by these scholars, and
2. the popular text now known as *Yoga-Vāsiṣṭha*.

Bhāskarakaṇṭha states in his *Ṭīkā* on *Īśvara-Pratyabhijñā-Vimarśinī* of Abhinavagupta:

> . . . *śrīmad-avatāra-kaṇṭha-putro bhāskara-kaṇṭho 'ham daśa-sahasrottara-lakṣa-saṁkhyāka-śrī-mokṣopāya-ṭīkā-karaṇena* . . .
>
> . . . I, Bhāskarakaṇṭha, son of Avatārakaṇṭha, having delved deep by writing a commentary on *Śrī-Mokṣopāya* consisting of 1,10,000 —vol. 1, p. 3

Hanneder (2005) gives a list of forty-two complete or incomplete manuscripts of both versions that have been found. There are also many shorter versions of *YV* the most well known of which is Abhinanda Gauḍa's *Laghu-Yoga-Vāsiṣṭha*. The details about the manuscripts of full and abridged versions may also be seen in Atreya (1936: 35-40), Hanneder (2006). Karmarkar (1956: i) mentions thirty-six manuscripts, many of them incomplete, and has consulted five for his work. The European scholars mentioned are also going into the depths to discover the *ur*-text. Our purpose in this publication is only to present *YV-BhG* in a readable translation.

Any study of *YV* would now be incomplete without making a close reference to the extensively detailed works of these scientific scholars in the field.

One of the greatest, the earliest, contributions to *YV* studies is by B.L. Atreya (1936: 6-8, 41-61 and appendices I to VI, pp. 660-717). He has shown the similarity of verses occurring in other classical texts to those of *YV* and has made an exhaustive list of the similarities with the minor Upaniṣads. These are indeed most interesting comparisons and the scholars will be hard put to decide as to who has borrowed from whom.

As these scholars are doing intensive and extensive work on the former version, we have contented ourselves with a dependence on the popular version. The full title, as published, is *Yoga-Vāsiṣṭha-Mahā-Rāmāyaṇa* (the Great *Rāmāyaṇa* that is Vasiṣṭha's Teaching on Yoga). In a number of verses in *YV* (I.1.52; I.2.9, 19) we find it called *Rāmāyaṇa*. Based on the story in chapter (*sarga*) 2 of the first section (*prakaraṇa*), *Rāmāyaṇa* has two sections, *Kathā-upāya* (the Story Method) and *Mokṣa-upāya* (the Method for Spiritual Liberation) (verse I.2.3). The text now commonly known as Vālmīki's *Rāmāyaṇa* is here called *Kathā-upāya*, and the one commonly known as this *Yoga-Vāsiṣṭha* (*YV*) is called *Mokṣa-upāya*. According to *YV*, the two put together is the complete *Rāmāyaṇa*.

This title for the text is confirmed elsewhere in *YV* also, for example, in a lengthy eulogy for the text (*YV* 3.8.8-17), a short excerpt is here:

Vasiṣṭha said:

> For those who hold self-knowledge as primary, O you of high intelligence, this alone is the supreme scripture among all scriptures, the beautiful great *Rāmāyaṇa* (*Mahā-Rāmāyaṇa*). Awakening proceeds from this best of narrative histories (*itihāsa*) being heard; it is stated to be the essence of all *itihāsas*. . . . What is here is elsewhere; what is not here is nowhere else. . . .[36]

---

36 What is here is elsewhere; what is not here is nowhere else: *yad ihāsti tad anyatra yan nehāsti na tat kvacit* — *Mahābhārata* 1.56.33 (critical edition 1997).

The background meaning of these terms will become clearer below in our brief summary of the chapter 2 of section I. The commentator ABS, in his commentary on I.2.3, calls the two sections *Pūrva-Rāmāyaṇa* (*Rāmāyaṇa*, First Part) in six cantos (*kāṇḍa*). Its further expansion (*upabṛṁhaṇa*) and complement is *Uttara-Rāmāyaṇa* (*Rāmāyaṇa*, Second Part). By the observance[37] of the First Part one gains the over-all purification (*pariśuddhi*) of the mind (*citta*) (ABS on I.2.8).

However, the chapter on "description of the count and so forth of the number of verses" (2.17) clearly states the title of the text to be *Mokṣa-upāya* (Means and Method for Spiritual Liberation). This is confirmed in numerous places such as VI.II.215.6 where the text is referred to as *Mokṣa-upāya*. VI.II.215.10 and especially verse 15 clearly state that the name of the text is *Mokṣābhyupāya* (Means and Method Towards Spiritual Liberation). The colophon at the end of each chapter throughout the text refers to it both as *Rāmāyaṇa* and *Mokṣa-upāya*.

There is also the question of how many verses comprise *YV*. Chapter II.17 gives these details. The colophon at the end of many chapters throughout the text says *dvātriṁśat-sāhasryāṁ saṁhitāyām* (in this text consisting of 32,000 verses). Our count of the published text shows the figures in the six sections (*prakaraṇa*) to be as follows:

1.	Vairāgya-prakaraṇa	1,146
2.	Mumukṣu-prakaraṇa	807
3.	Utpatti-prakaraṇa	5,383
4.	Sthiti-prakaraṇa	2,414
5.	Upaśama-prakaraṇa	4,279

---

[37] *Anuṣṭhāna*. In the traditions of India one may undertake the study (*svādhyāya*) of a sacred text, or listening to a recitation by a preceptor, a certain number of times in a definite period, with certain rules of sanctity. These observances are still very widely held and often by tens of thousands of people together at a time.

6.	Nirvāṇa-prakaraṇa, Part 1	5,288
	Nirvāṇa-prakaraṇa, Part 2	8,802
	Total	28,119[38]

According to Karmarkar (1956: iii) the count is 29,300.

YV, however, in chapter 17 of the second section (Mumukṣu-prakaraṇa) gives the following counts:

Vairāgya-prakaraṇa	1,500
Mumukṣu-Vyavahāra-prakaraṇa	1,000
Utpatti-prakaraṇa	7,000
Sthiti-prakaraṇa	3,000
Upa-Śānti (Upaśama)-prakaraṇa	5,000
Nirvāṇa-prakaraṇa	14,500
Total	32,000

The text does not actually give the number of verses in the last *prakaraṇa* but it is calculated by ABS, the commentator, on the basis of the statement in 2.17.41.

The title of this chapter is Grantha-Saṁkhyādi-Varṇanam, (description of the count and so forth of the number of verses); by "so forth" is indicated the fact that for each *prakaraṇa* the text gives few lines of indication of the content or subject matter.

Of these, 267 verses are in Arjuna-Upākhyāna (*YV-BhG*) as compared to 700 verses of *MB-BhG*, with additional verses in the Kāśmīrī recension of the same.

The part of *YV* presented here is titled Arjunopākhyāna (AU) in *Yoga-Vāsiṣṭha* (*YV*) but the commentator ABS refers to it as *Bhagavad-Gītā* (*YV-BhG*) perhaps to show its connection with the *Bhagavad-Gītā* as found in *Mahābhārata* (*MB-BhG*). Following ABS we refer to our presentation as *YV-BhG*.

---

38 I am grateful to Pandit Chandramani for having provided the count.

A number of commentaries on *YV* are known, for example, *Vasiṣṭha-Rāmāyaṇa-Candrikā* by Advayānanda, *Bhāṣya* by Gaṅgādharendra, *Pada-Candrikā* by Mādhava Sarasvatī and of course ABS that we have depended on. Hanneder (2006: 11) mentions the commentaries by Mahīdhara, Pūrṇānanda and Paramānanda Miśra. As recognized by Hanneder (2006: 47), K.C. Pandey (2000: 29) states:

> His [Abhinavagupta's] commentary on the *Yoga-Vāsiṣṭha*. We have no other source of information about it than a tradition current among Kāśmīrian Paṇḍits.[39]

Karmarkar (1956) mentions manuscripts of the commentaries by Ātmasukha and Mummaḍideva on the Arjuna-Upākhyāna section.

The title of the commentary by ABS is *Tātparya-Prakāśa* (the Illumination of the Essence). He pays homage to his guru lineage, naming, in that order, Sarvajña Sarasvatī (verse 12), Rāmānanda Muni (verse 14) and Gaṅgādharendra (verse 18). What their mutual relationship is not explained there but no need, the *puṣpikā* (colophon) at the end of *Tātparya-Prakāśa* is clear:

> This work is composed by the monk (*bhikṣu*) named Śrīmad-ānanda-Bodhendra Sarasvatī, disciple of the monk named Gaṅgādharendra Sarasvatī (who was the) disciple at the venerable feet of Śrī Rāmacandra Sarasvatī who was the disciple at the venerable feet of Sarvajña Sarasvatī. . . .

[39] We have in our possession an Urdu translation of the abridged version of *YV* in Farsi by Dara Shikoh, tr. Abu Alhan, published by Khuda Baksh Oriental Public Library, Patna, 1992. We have not found reference to Arjunopākhyāna content in this summary. For references to other translations in Farsi and Urdu, etc., see Atreya (1936: 31-33, 40); Hanneder (2005: 145ff.). Also see reproductions of paintings from Farsi manuscripts in Hanneder (2005: 143) and Krause-Stinner (2011: lxxiii ff.).

Thus the order of monks is Sarvajña Sarasvatī, whose disciple was Rāmacandra Sarasvatī, whose disciple was Gaṅgādharendra, the guru of the author of *Tātparya-Prakāśa.*

Among the five closing verses of the commentary, the fourth one reads:

r̥tu-rasa-turaga-mahī 1766 śaka-vikāri-śubha-vatsarasya śiśirartau ।
phālguna-sīta-saptamyām bhr̥gu-rauhīṇa-varṣake siddham ॥

giving us the date of the completion of the work as 7th day of the bright fortnight of Phālguna month in the Śaka era 1766, year named Vikāri.[40] This is equivalent of Friday, 14 March 1845 CE.[41]

As has been noted by other scholars, *YV* contains verses similar to other texts, including the *Bhagavad-Gītā* as found in *Mahābhārata* (*MB-BhG*) even outside the Narrative of Arjuna, Arjunopākhyāna (*YV-BhG*). For example:

nāsato vidyate bhāvo nābhāvo vidyate sataḥ ।

There is no being of non-existent unreal; there is no non-being of existent real. — *YV* 6.II.213.10 and *MB-BhG* 2.16

The same half verse also occurs in *YV-BhG* 6.I.54.7 (3.7 in our version).

Similarly, as noted above, the verses 6.II.214.14-17 spoken by Rāma in final surrender to Vasiṣṭha echo *MB-BhG* verses spoken by Arjuna to Kr̥ṣṇa and statements of Kr̥ṣṇa also. Numerous such examples can be given but that would be a digression from the purpose of the current presentation.

The translation of *YV-BhG* being offered here would not be possible without taking the help of *TP* of ABS who has delved

---

40 Like the well-known system of names of weekdays and months, the Indian system has names of years in a sixty-year cycle.

41 I am grateful to Pandit Chandramani and Dinesh Sharma for this conversion from the Śaka era date to the common era date.

deep into the meanings of obscure words and into the profound philosophical aspects of the teaching offered in *YV-BhG*. This indeed with the reservation expressed by other scholars that ABS forces the text to be read as closely Vedāntic as possible, neglecting the views of many other schools incorporated. The commentary of ABS is dated at least a millennium after the composition of *YV* and is tinged with the interpretations based on Śaṅkara's Vedānta, which is somewhat far-fetched as a true interpretation of the contents of *YV*, the commentary is helpful in unravelling a number of words and phrases. The philosophy presented in *TP* is by no means loyal to the original philosophical intents of *YV* which is its own *siddhānta*, its own philosophical system; some arguments of which coincide with those of other schools such as Kāśmīr Śaivism, Buddhist Vijñānavāda or Śaṅkara's Advaita. A full statement of the philosophy of *YV* is yet to be made by someone with both profound scholarship and spiritual experience.

About the versions of *MB-BhG*, so far, two versions, or recensions, have been popularly known. (1) The one found in *MB* on which Śaṅkarācārya and others have written commentaries. (2) Kashmir recension which has many variant readings and additional verses, on which Abhinavagupta and Rāmakaṇṭha have written commentaries. *YV-BhG* has been translated before as part of the full translations of *YV* and separately by Karmarkar (1956) but had not been known widely. Now a new translation is being presented here. Some day a scholar might like to compare the three versions as to the philosophical implications of the variants. It would be interesting to compare the variant readings of the Arjunopākhyāna section in Bhāskarakaṇṭha's commentary on *Mokṣopāya*, if it were to be found in some manuscripts, but we see that Bruno Lo Turco (2011) edition of the same begins with chapter 195 of Nirvāṇa-Prakaraṇa, thus missing the Arjunopākhyana section. It would be interesting for scholars to see translations of the commentaries on Arjunopākhyāna by Ātmasukha and Mummaḍideva as mentioned by Karmarkar (1956: ii-iii). He has also shown the important variant readings from these manuscripts in his edition. We have not found any significant suggestions to the intent of *YV-BhG* in the variants cited in Karmarkar; other scholars may hold a different opinion. Few examples will suffice here:

52.33. *deho* > *dehī*. He will be a body > he will be a body-owner.

52.35. He will enlighten [Arjuna] . . . with arguments and methods (*yuktibhiḥ*).

53.16. *niḥ-saṅgas tvam yathā-prāpta-karmavān na ni-badhyase brahmārpita-samācāro brahmaiva bhavasi kṣaṇāt*. Free of attachments, performing the acts as one comes across them, you will not be bound. > Good conduct surrendered to *Brahman*, you become *Brahman* within a moment.

53.18. *sarva-bhūtātmā* > *sarva-bhāvātmā*. The very self of all beings > the very self of all states of being.

53.30. *iti jñāta-vibhāgasya buddhau tasya pari-grahaḥ* > *iti jñānād vi-bhāgo 'sya yo dvaitasya pari-kṣayaḥ*. For one who has understood this division, it [then] vanishes in the *buddhi*. > Thus it is a division from knowledge that is the diminution of duality.

54.4. *sparśa-mātrākhyā mātrā-sparśa-bhramātmakaḥ* > *spanda-mātrākhyā kalāsmin paramātmani*. There remains merely a touch of the matter consisting of an illusion of [this] touch of matter. > There remains in this supreme self the aspect (*kalā*) that is called mere vibration (*spanda*).

55.5. *āsaktim āhuḥ kartṛtvam* > *asaktim āhur a-kartṛtvam*. Attraction (attachment) is called doership > non-attachment is called non-doership.

55.33. *api sphuṭati vindhyādrau* > *api sphuṭati vidhy-aṇḍe*. Even when Vindhya mountain is exploding. > Even when the universe-egg is exploding.

56.21. *nānānubhavanātmani* > *nānā-bhuvana-nāmāni*. Today has vanishd in the mind-kingdom that consisted of many experiences. . . . > Today has vanished in the mind-kingdom that had the names of many worlds. . . .

57.7. *brahmaṇi brahmaṇāmbaram* > *brahmaṇi brahma cāvaram*. This cutting and splitting of cloth in *Brahman* by *Brahman* . . . > This cutting and splitting of lower *Brahman* in *Brahman*. . . .

58.13. *bhava vi-bhavo bhagavān bhiyām a-bhūmiḥ* > *bhava vi-rājo bhuvanaika-nātha-mūrtiḥ*. Become enriched with variety of powers as a blessed one (*Bhagavān*), no [more a] ground of fears. > Become free of *rajas*, unitary image of the Lord of the universe.

Our work here suffers from such imperfections as:

1. The verses in the Appendix 1 should have been translated, but that would be part of a study of comparison of the three versions suggested above.
2. In the narratives of some of the summarized stories the exact chapter and verse reference is missing. These were transcriptions from lectures given from memory over many decades.
3. The commentaries of Ātmasukha and Mummaḍideva (manuscripts in the Bhandarkar Oriental Research Institute, Pune, vide Karmarkar (1956: ii-iii) should have been compared with ABS.

Whatever is accurate here belongs to the sages; whatever is faulty is mine.

Summary Paraphrase of Arjunopākhyāna

1. Only some salient points of the teaching are being included here. For full teaching, please see the translation of the text.
2. The summaries of verses and ideas identical or similar to *MB-BhG* mostly have not been included.

THE narrative of *YV-BhG* takes place in the context of the spatio-temporal zones within spatio-temporal zones and all that within the timeless and spaceless realms of pure consciousness like "a great sky within a sky" (*YV* 6.I.52.11). The cosmic events such as creations and dissolutions of universes, suns and planets all take place as nothing different from the Supreme Transcendent as bangles and bracelets are not different from gold within this realm of "cosmic bracelets". Consciousness devolves into the forms of forces controlling different functions; these devolutions are the controlling deities. They set the laws for the governance of societies stating "what is acceptable and what rejectable" (ibid. 15) norms of thoughts, acts and behaviours.

Of these, Yama (the lord of laws and justice and death) tires of "killing" the beings. As expiations, he sometimes undertakes different time durations of ascesis refraining from such "violence" and the earth becomes overcrowded.

[*Comment*: Vasiṣṭha the preceptor sage here is a *trikāla-darśin* (one who sees in all three realms of time). Here he is teaching in Tretā-yuga about the events that will occur at the end of Dvāpara-yuga.[1]]

---

[1] The Hindu time scale counts a single creation era to be 4,328 years. →

In one of the dimensions of these multi-layer time-fields, then, the Earth Deity will approach and beseech Viṣṇu (the All-preserving Lord). He, listening to her prayers, will incarnate on earth in a dual form. One form is one pretending to be ignorant and the other the Lord in His full glory of transcendent Self-awareness. Thus His one body, the former, is Vāsudeva or Kṛṣṇa, son of Vasudeva, and the other, latter, is Arjuna the son of Pāṇḍu.

A war will ensue between the five Pāṇḍava brothers and their cousins led by Duryodhana over the kingdom. Eighteen *akṣauhiṇī*[2] armies will perish in the war lasting eighteen days. Thereby, Viṣṇu will reduce the burden on the earth.

But the Lord's ignorant *avatāra*, Arjuna, will become saddened and depressed at the prospect of such a war. So, to fulfil His current purpose on earth the Lord, with his awake, transcendent Self-aware body, will give him the teachings of the highest reality: One is neither born nor dies. The perennial, unborn, eternal self is not killed when the body is killed. When the inner self is subtler than even space, is infinite and of a nature of unity, what can be destroyed, what can vanish?

→ Similarly an equal period of dissolution, for our particular world. That is the most common count but there are schools that contract or expand the period by many zeros. For example, if we were to interpret these as years of the *deva* worlds, the duration of a creation era would be 43,210 human years. One creation era is divided into fourteen Manu intervals; each of which again into seventy-one *catur-yuga* (aeon-quartets) each containing four *yuga*s (aeons). In the current creation epoch this is the seventh Manu interval and we are into its twenty-eighth *catur-yuga* period. The Tretā and Dvāpara *yuga*s, spoken of in this narrative, are in the current *catur-yuga* period. The *Mahābhārata* War occurred at the end of last Dvāpara era and at the start of the current Kali era (dark ages).

2 One *akṣauhiṇī* army consists of 21,870 elephant-riders; 21,870 chariots; 65,610 cavalry and 1,09,350 infantry; total 2,18,700 warriors. So, eighteen *akṣauhiṇī*s consisted of 39,36,600 warriors of both sides that are said to have perished in the eighteen-day war.

Different organs and faculties, each performs its function. Then when all acts are being performed by this collective, it is laughable that one may claim a doership singly attributed to one's ego?

[*Comment*: This point is similar to the Buddhist view that in the *puggala* (*pudgala*), personality composition, it is the constituents that perform all the functions and there is no other inner self. However, here, there is clearly an inner self that is immortal and subtler than even space but one is not to entertain the claims of ego.]

One should adhere to one's duties and perform all actions surrendered to Divinity. That "I" and the universe is all *Brahman* — holding this contemplation at all times is the true surrender to Divinity. All of this world and the sentiment "I" are a mere flicker arising in the infinite Consciousness giving an appearance of being separate from the same even though non-separate.

The way we insist on the separateness, often there arises in us a sense of unity of it all; why do we not grasp that sense and hold on to it? Why do we keep insisting on the variety of concepts (*vikalpa*).

> Awareness-as-self (*bodhātman*) is indeed the meaning of (all) words. The universe is one, there is no doubt about it. I am the expectations, I the universe, I the reflexive self,[3] I too the action. I am time, I am non-dual, I am the dual, I also am the universe. Let your mind be fixed on Me, my devotee, worshipping me, bow to Me. Thus uniting the Self in yoga, intent upon Me, you will come only to Me.
>
> — 53.32-34

[*Comment*: The verses seem to echo the *MB-BhG* in tenth chapter titled Vibhūti-Yoga (Yoga of the Diversity of Divine Powers) and the eleventh titled Viśva-Rūpa-Darśana (Showing the Universe Form of the Lord). However, there the Lord speaks of his manifold

3 *Svam* (the personality), a possession of the true self. The word is often used in a reflexive-possessive sense, as *svo dehaḥ* (own body), *svam riktham* (own wealth). Whatever is my own, *svam*, that I the self am, therefore what can be "mine"?

powers in the immanent universe. Here the Lord speaks as absolute, transcendent *Brahman*. This is by way of instruction to Arjuna that he, too, should dwell in the realization of the same Consciousness.]

In this context Kṛṣṇa explains that He has two forms, the immanent and the transcendent. Arjuna may begin with worshipping the Incarnate form but use that only as a stepping stone towards the Absolute Transcendent.

> When I say, "I am this" and "I am this", I am only teaching you the meaning of the essential *ātman* (*ātma-tattva*) as your own true being. — 53.41

> "One" is the meaning of the word "All". The meaning of "one" is *ātman* the self. — 53.45

The flavour and taste in all the juices and waters and milk of all kinds; the subtle experience of being within oneself; like butter (*ghee*) inside all different kinds of milk; brilliance inside and outside of all gems; [all one] space in a thousand jars; a single thread joining a thousand pearls; in all objects and entities, in a hundred thousand bodies from Brahmā (the deity of one cosmos) to a blade of grass — it is this *ātman* the self. Who in this kills or is killed?

Like a mirror neutral towards the reflected images, not destroyed upon their destruction — so it is this *ātman* the self. When I say "I am this" and "I am not this", know that what I am explaining is that I am the self of all. You be the same.

As the rock nature of all mountains, wood nature of all trees, the nature of water itself unaltered through all modifications of fickle ripples, gold in all bracelets — it is this *ātman* the self in all entities and objects.

The saintly wander the earth liberated-while-living (*jīvanmukta*), their being in evenness and equanimity — they are the ones who reach the unmodifiable highest state.

There is no reality to pains and pleasures. One who dwells evenly towards pains and pleasures is qualified for immortal status, because *ātman* the self does not bloom with pleasures and does not wither with pains. The Consciousness-self (*cetana-ātman*), though taking the appearance of "apprehensible" and the "apprehension consciousness", the mind and the like are unconscious in themselves and have entered an equally unconscious physical frame. When all this diminishes, nothing of *ātman* diminishes. Make all this *Brahman* to be one with *Brahman*. You are the *Brahman*-ocean.

This does not mean that you abandon your current duties. The way a *khaṇḍa-vāta* (wind confined to the limits of a cave) may appear a separate entity and performs its function in the cave — so do you perform your acts while dwelling in the body-cave. Perform your actions as you happen to come across the duties and necessities and thus be an ornament to the earth.

Do not imagine self in non-self and non-self in the self. At the loss of the body, nothing is lost. The only loss would be the loss of *ātman* the self but *ātman* is never lost, never vanishes.

Arjuna asks: What then is the meaning of people being convinced of death? And what is meaning of heaven and hell? (55.17). The reply is given as follows:

The *jīva* (live self), dwelling in the bodies, is but an aggregate network consisting of five subtle elements — earth, water, fire, air and space. This one is tugged at and pulled by *vāsanās*, propensities formed of past actions suffused into the subtle body and stays in the body like a bird in a cage. The powers of hearing, sight, touch, taste and smell blow around like the wind blows smells about. The body is no more than what consists of these *vāsanās*; it is of no other stratagem. It diminishes and vanishes when one has renounced *vāsanās* and then one attains the pedestal [indicated in the teachings by the word] That.[4] It is by the force of *vāsanās* that this *jīva* wanders in diverse bodies of species like a person in magic show whirling about in sky.

---

4 As in the *mantras* like *tat savitur vareṇyam* and the super-sentences like *tat tvam asi*.

The *jīva* under the power of *vāsanā*s takes with him the natures of the senses and wanders like the wind blowing a smell from the flower, to migrate. Then the [previous] body no longer stirs as the *jīva* has abandoned it like a tree standing still when the breeze is quiet. The lifeless body following natural laws deteriorates and becomes invisible. This they call death.

Wherever in the space of consciousness or the material space, the *jīva* sees (visualizes and creates), according to the habit of its *vāsanā*s, that very form extended. The (abandoned) body is then viewed by the *jīva* as non-existent; so also, you, too, should see it like a person (does not see the body) in sleep.

Whatever *bhāvanā*, brought to being by projecting a will, was generated at the first quick instant of creation, that alone carries forward till dissolution.

With an effort being made today the reality created yesterday is altered the way a house built yesterday may be burnt to ashes today and the seeds of non-virtue generated yesterday may be annulled by expiations of today. Whoever puts in the full and strong human effort (*puruṣārtha*) with a continuity before and after, from past into the future, attains victory in a moment.

[*Comment*: This is a central point of the teachings of *YV* that one can create or attain anything by the human effort of will and persistence, *puruṣārtha* or *pauruṣa*.]

Even if the Vindhya[5] mountain is exploding and the world-dissolution-wind is blowing, the effort of one's human will (*pauruṣa*), applied in accordance with the scriptural teachings, remains paramount. It should, therefore, never be abandoned by a wise person.

One's intelligence marred by the ancient delusion, one sees all heaven and hell and the like according to the long practised habit of one's *vāsanā*s. This *vāsanā* remains effective and ingrained only

---

5 Before the rise of the Himalayas, Vindhyas formed the boundary between north and south India, and were regarded as the epitome of strength.

because of long habitual practice but it is like a dream and therefore one should make all effort at diminishing and vanquishing it.

But, from what does this *vāsanā* arise and how is it to be diminished? — asks Arjuna. He is advised: It arises from idiocy of delusion, this imposition of "self" on non-self. It is dissolved by the force of great awakening that is self-knowledge. Arjuna, you have already cultivated yourself, and, truly, you have gained experiential knowledge (*vijñāna*). Now, just abandon the *vāsanā* concepts such as "this", "I am that", "these people", "by me", etc.

When *vāsanā* is dissolved, the individuated consciousness, *jīva*, is also dissolved by itself, and time and space are cancelled. That being the case then, who is it that comes to the total elimination of relativities and who then attains the supreme bliss? — Arjuna asks. The Lord replies: The true nature of oneself becomes confused only by one's own *saṅkalpa* (the intentional volition) the same taking the form of *vāsanā* becomes an individuated self, *jīva*. When, however one is re-awakened to one's own nature that is non-dependent, non-intentional, immutable, the true self-form, that is called *mokṣa* (liberation). One who is freed of the reins of *vāsanā*, right in this very life, is called *mukta* (free liberated). Do see this reality.

One who is not yet freed of *vāsanā*, no matter how many virtuous acts he performs, and no matter how all-knowing he may become, he is still bound from all sides, like a bird in a cage. One who realizes that this *vāsanā* is like the sight of peacock feathers in empty space in front of one's bad eyes, he becomes liberated right here, for, *vāsanā* alone is bondage and its vanquishing is freedom (*mokṣa*).

O Arjuna, become liberated-while-living by freeing yourself of the *vāsanā*s. Thus attaining the inner coolness, abandon this sorrow regarding the (death of) kinsmen. Having no doubt as to the impossibility of decay and death, your inner receptacle of dispositions clear like space, abandoning all intentions regarding desirables and undesirables, become devoid of the colourings of attachments.

Whatever duties of your own come your way in the flow, performing those, one remains liberated-while-living. "I abandon this act", "I undertake this initiative", all this decision-making is a form of deluded and stupefied (*mūḍha*) mind. A knowing one's state is an even one.

Those whose minds are pacified, who are liberated-while-living, continue to stir in the world like one stirring while asleep. They withdraw their senses from the objects of senses like a turtle pulling in its limbs and remain in a state of stillness and stability.

> In the universal spirit-mind, the painter of mind-image(s) creates a mural without a wall — the universe with three worlds, divided into three divisions of time. In the empty sky, made even of (empty) space, (painted) clear with pastels of *vr̥ttis*, in the beginning of creation, Oh, a strange painting was first spread out by mind, the painter! A splendid painting was first made, and then the wall, which is space, was created; Oh, what confusion! Unique is this great magic, the excessive *māyā*, this beautiful magic of a wall made of straw. There is not the slightest difference between the two objects of apprehension, the wall and the mural, as these walls are experienced arising in the very painting in the mind. Know those walls even more void than empty space as both the creation and dissolution of the world pass confusing in the mind within a moment. — 56.8-12

All that we experience of the world and a misapprehension of ourselves is all a play of mind-kingdom (*mano-rājya*). All the universes and so forth are like figures (*putrikā*) in the painting of the mind on the mind. The way a cloud is illuminated by the sun and then by the power of the very illuminating sun it also vanishes, so it is with the delusion we have about the universes being real.

> There being no walls (for this mural) the three worlds and so forth have no forms outside (the mind); neither they nor you exist (as separate individual reality). What is made to cease? By whom?
> — 56.16

As in the mind of someone suddenly surprised, all kinds of worlds arise and vanish in a moment, so also it is with our perception of the worlds. This mind is capable of converting a micro-instant into an aeon and changing the little into much. So, also it turns non-being into being. It is thus that all this confusion has arisen and we attribute to it an adamantine solidity. But, when we know that all this adamantine reality is produced by the flash of imagination (*pratibhā*), and the wisdom is simply reversing that flash, whether engaging in or disengaging from the world, then where is the adamantine concreteness of the universe?

Oh, how entertaining and of beautiful colours is this world, so clear, attractive to the sight, with many lines drawn in the ink of darkness (*tamas*), colourful with the rays of many splendours. With many limbs of the cycles (of creation, *kalpa*s) and their parts (*yuga*s, aeons), painted with colours of many attractions (*rāga*s), rich with the luxury of many views, interesting for its many experiences.

With the fierce splendour of many celestial bodies, with many forms in east and west, with blooming lotuses of stars, moon and sun in the blue lake of the sky.

With the vines and leaves of rows of clouds arranged in diverse designs, puppet-images of celestial beings, *asura*s and men drawn in the chambers of the three worlds, its sky-walls white-washed with most brilliant light of the sun and moon, this world is a theatre.

In the very space, genius alone her theatre, young, innocent-looking, colouring all loci with whirling wheels (*cakra*s) of the lights of consciousness alone; fervent in her play, this dancing girl, the triad of worlds, charming to the mind, is created by the sensual painter, *cittaka*[6] (the Mind).

The (slim) vine of whose (body and) limbs is the golden mountain, clouds the braids of her hair; looking at the worlds by moving her eyes, the moon and the sun, wearing for garments the

---

6 A play on words here. Citraka would be a painter; here this painter "this little mind" is *cittaka*.

scriptures that maintain control through (the instruction of) *dharma*, *artha* and *kāma*; the seven lower worlds (*pātāla*s) her legs and the lofty earth her hips.

She is strong with four arms — Brahmā, Indra, Śiva and Viṣṇu; her slim body has full quivering breasts covered with the bodice of harmony (*sattva*); the very earth enwrapped by beautiful snakes (*kuṇḍalinī*) is her lotus seat (*mūlādhāra cakra*). She has the great middle world for her midriff, with its mountains for leafy drawings.

The glances of her eyes stop the stirrings and shiftings of night's darkness,

1. with stars for the thrill of her body-hair, lightning for rows of teeth;
2. her bristling of hair, the (birth of) incomparable beings and fourteen worlds quivering;
3. wearing the winds of dissolution for *kadamba* (*Nauclea cadamba*) flowers.

> Endowed with life, this wonder has been created in (empty) space, consisting of (empty) space alone. By mind, the maker of strange and durable pictures, expert in the art of refined painting is created this beautiful maiden, the world-trio, attractive (for her) many dalliances and graces. — 56.28-37

Oh, what wonder the assumed "reality" of this world is. One sees a wall stretched out in a painting done on non-wall. What magic! It is as if to say, "an empty gourde sank and a rock floated".

The *YV* text here repeats the word *vyoman* many times over. The word literally means "space", "sky" and by implication empty nature. The commentator ABS even uses the expression *śūnya-ātman* (the very self of space-like void, the void-self). When the three worlds consist of the very self of space, whence is this arising of space-ness of I-ness? All this universe is void created in the void. The void dissolves in the void. In void, void is being experienced; in void, the void is expanded. This very idea may be literally translated thus: All this universe is empty space created in the empty space. The empty space dissolves in the empty space. In empty space, empty space is being experienced; in empty space, the empty space is expanded.

[*Comment*: Even though this appears to be the Buddhist teaching, it does not deny but affirms that the ultimate reality is *ātman* and *Brahman*. It is to be borne in mind that there are still Hindu denominations that worship *śūnya-Brahman*.[7] The topic of *śūnya* in Vedic–Hindu thought has been the subject of many deep studies.

This long, groaning world of migrations, *saṁsāra*, is coiled around by the rope of *vāsanā* like a string of long creation (process). By uncoiling the *vāsanā* alone is this (world) uncoiled here, Arjuna.

As a reflection in the mirror, so it is in *Brahman* Itself. It is not subject to being cut and burst since there is no "otherness" that will cut its opposite "another". Such an absence of *vāsanā*s has arisen in you through an awakening because one who is not free of *vāsanā*s, no matter how many virtuous acts he performs, he is like a lion confined to a cage.

If one has the slightest seed of *vāsanā* left, it grows into a big forest of *saṁsāra* in the ground of consciousness. When it is burnt through repeated practice with the fire of truth ablaze, then, having been thus burnt it never grows again. The burnt seed of *vāsanā*s no longer makes one sink into the objects of the world; one then remains clear and pure in the face of pleasures and pains and becomes like lotus petal in the water.

Arjuna is conclusively advised:

Tranquil of self,
all fears gone,
having abandoned all the immeasurable expectations,
blown out (nirvāṇa),
all the great delusion of the mind melted away,

---

[7] For example, the Mahimā sect of Odisha who believes in *Śūnya-Brahman*.

having apprehended this purifying knowledge of accuracy completely,
having rejected the possibility of killing and such,
now abide in the self, a being of singular unified peace. — 57.12

Here Arjuna declares his spiritual ascent in a verse identical to *MB-BhG* (18.73): My delusion has vanished. I have regained my mindfulness and remembrance of ultimate reality. It has happened by Thy grace, O Infallible One. I am now stabilized and stilled, free of doubts. I shall proceed to do in accord with your advice.

The Lord reiterates and summarizes his teaching. If the operations of the mind have become pacified through awakening right within the heart, that mind has achieved an inward calm and purity of *sattva* has arrived.

Here is that inward Consciousness without an object of consciousness (*cetya*). It is freed, leaving behind no residue. It is the All that proceeds from All. Those stuck on the ground and so forth do not know of this state which is like that of a bird that has flown high in the sky. This inward Consciousness is luminous, pure, free of intentionality, not approachable, this self, far from the sight of the physical eye.

The *vāsanā* not purified prevents the vision and cannot see that highest pedestal which is clear and pure, beyond all things. The worldly view cannot observe it just like people cannot see atomic particles. That upon attainment of which all these exterior objects, jars and cloths, vanish; there, in the transcendent pedestal, what will poor *vāsanā* do? How could it ever prevail again?

It is like a tiny snowflake vanishing in a volcano when this little *vāsanā* insignificant like a particle has encountered the pure essence of Consciousness. How can it then bind anyone to the ties of experiences [arising from karmic cycles]? How can the full network of the world stand before the ample and powerful wind of the Essence that is Consciousness. The nescience prevails and flashes about only so long as the pure self is not fully known by the self itself.

Then, all views concerning objects of sight vanish and only purity arises. It is when the own-self (*sva-ātman*), that is fulfiller and filler of all, that makes all beings and entities full and complete, that one has come to a pure state like that of the sky.

Having the form of nature of wholeness, yet devoid of all forms and configurations, the transcendent reality beyond the reach of words — with what can it ever be compared?

The final words of the Lord are:

> Therefore, give up this poisonous infection of objects and experiences (*viṣaya-viṣa-viṣūcikā*), throwing aside expertly the *vāsanā* of the stagnation in I-ness.
>
> By means of the secret antidote-*mantra*[8] of contemplation, become free of the worldly being (*vibhava*), a blessed lord, no further ground for fears and dangers. — 58.13

Here, Vasiṣṭha tells Rāma that when the lord of the three worlds will have spoken thus, Arjuna will remain silent for a moment like a honeybee on the tip of a blue lotus and then Arjuna will say:

> This my intelligence has reached the highest ascendance, Lord, with all the weight of grief completely dissolved by the words of you, who are the master of the worlds. It is like a lily awakened by the sun, the Lord of the day. — 58.15

8 This refers to controlling snakes and the cure of any poisoning by the power of *mantras*.

Chapter I

The Narrative of the Incarnation of Nara and Nārāyaṇa

[*Comment*: Now is being explained the renunciation of ego consisting of abandoning attachment, also, the realities of one to be worshipped, to be known, arranged together with differences of conditions.[1] The world is a dream of the *jīva*, it vanishes by absence of attachment towards it; therefore Vasiṣṭha introduces the narrative of Arjuna.[2]]

Vasiṣṭha said:

1. That which is from the beginning the dream of *jīva*,[3] soft with many tender experiences,[4] know this worldly cycle (*saṁsāra*[5]) to be neither real nor unreal.[6]

---

1 Opening verse by the commentator.

2 The commentator begins his commentary on each chapter with an introductory verse.

3 *Jīva* (individuated life-principle, the individual soul which is a spark of the universal self). Because of this special connotation the Sanskrit term is used without translating it.

4 *Kalana*, from the verb root *kal*, is difficult to translate since it conveys: to calculate (as in *kāla*, meaning time) to count, to make sweet sound, to assume, to observe, to think of, to put on, to regard or consider, to undergo, to be influenced by, to perform and so forth. The word "experience" in our translation should connote all of these meanings.

5 *Saṁsāra* (the cycle of worldly involvements and transmigrations); the opposite of *nirvāṇa* or *mokṣa* (liberation). From hereon the Sanskrit term will be used.

6 Literally, neither true nor consisting of unreality, or, neither existence nor non-existence. The ontological "reality" is inseparable from →

[*Comment*: A dream is different for every individual; constitution of objects in wakefulness is shared by all. How can it be called a dream, being experienced at the same time by all and separate from dreams? The answer is given: That dream which is the first dream from the beginning of the collective self of all *jīva*s, know that to be this *saṁsāra*, (world of transmigrations) imagined as our wakeful experience.]

2. The *jīva* cannot ever have a dream like an (ordinary) person, so, these phases of wakefulness here are definitely producers of the wakeful dream.[7]

[*Comment*: Why is it imagined in this way, since a dream other than that of individuals belonging to the collective is not known? (The answer is that) our phases of past, present and so forth, known to us during wakefulness, arise, in fact, from both wakefulness (which is our level of experience) and dream, and are thus inseparable from the dream state.

3. Know this dream of *jīva* to be long, as it does not appear (to end) quickly. It is indeed unreal, there being no substance to it, O best among the knowers of what ought to be known.

[*Comment*: Being untrue (*asatya*) and a non-entity or unreality (*a-vastu*), it is obviously a dream but it seems different in nature from (what we call normal) dream. The reason for this experience of difference between the two is: Our dreams end very quickly and for this reason we know them to be untrue; however, the dream of the collective *jīva*

→ epistemological "truth" and the words *sat* and *satya* denote both without differentiating between the two.

[7] *Jāgrat-svapna*, fourth of the seven states of consciousness taught elsewhere in *YV*. Also one of the nine states as taught in Kāśmīr Śaivism. Inquire for our audio-recordings on *Śiva-Sūtras* from ahymsinpublishers@gmail.com

goes on for a long time and therefore seems different from our kinds of dream.]

4. As it were, going from one dream to another, the little *jīva*s after *jīva*s see only untruth, because their truth is beclouded, O sinless one.

5. Unconsciousness[8] in the conscious and in the unconscious the suffering of the conscious; reality in unreality (arises) because of the delusion of the experience of each individual *jīva*.

   [*Comment*: Seeing the opposition of the natures of entities and states (*vastu-svabhāva-vaiparītya*) also the dreamness (of the wakeful worldly experiences is proved, as follows): In the *ajaḍa*, not-unconscious but the full, conscious *Brahman*, there is (the appearance of the) unconscious (states such as our) past and present universe; and in the unconscious *ahaṅkāra* (ego, body, etc.) there is an attributing of consciousness, because the identity of self is falsely imposed on them. This arises from the error or delusion called the experience of the individual *jīva*s, who are within just a small part of the collective *jīva*.]

6. Seeing even inside one (spiritual) sun, the entire delusion of three worlds, the *jīva*s wander about lost in dreams with a chain of (one false idea after another of imagined) differentiations.

   [*Comment*: The *jīva*s wander in confusion through the chain of imaginings of differentiations.]

7. Because the (collective) *jīva* is all-pervading and infinite, even though the *jīva*s are living (in individuality), whatever

---

[8] *Jaḍa* is unconscious by nature and not temporarily so. Matter is *jaḍa* whereas *jīva* is conscious; not *jaḍa* but *ajaḍa*. It is by error that *jīva* begins to identify itself with the ego and body which are material.

they contemplate[9] or become aware of, they immediately (experience) as if it were a truth and reality (*satya*).

[*Comment*: He explains the reason why they attribute reality and truth to imagined differentiations: Even though it becomes a *jīva* through individuation, it is transcendentally all-pervading, endless true and real through non-differentiation. As such whatever they (the *jīva*s) contemplate (do *bhāvanā* of), to the same they quickly wake up, become aware of. When the *jīva*s give up attachment to that imaginary world, then the illusion of its reality is turned off and the *jīva*, having become enlightened (*buddha*) as to the real essence, attains liberation while still living in the body (*jīvan-mukti*).]

8-9. Embracing the beautiful way of non-attachment taught by the lotus-eyed (Kṛṣṇa), O mighty-armed one, embracing which the great meditative, liberated while alive (*jīvan-mukta*), Pāṇḍu's son, by name Arjuna, will without trouble renounce his comfortable life, making it pain-free (*nir-duḥkha*). So should you renounce your own life.

[*Comment*: To explain the above he now embarks on Arjuna narrative. Pain-free (*sukha, nir-duḥkha*) because of entering into the state of being liberated while living (*jīvan-mukta*).]

Rāma said:

10. O Brāhmaṇa (Vasiṣṭha), when will that son of Pāṇḍu, Arjuna, be born? What kind of teaching of non-attachment will Viṣṇu give to him?

Vasiṣṭha said:

11. "Is" (*asti*), "Essence alone" (*san-mātram*), "Self" (*ātman*);

---

[9] *Bhāvayanti*. This is formed in causative mood of the verb root *bhū*, to be. The noun *bhāvanā* formed in this mood of *bhū* if often used for contemplation, sentiment, to bring about a change in oneself through such contemplation or sentiment. In this verse it means "they bring about into being by imagining, contemplating, dwelling on".

— even though assuming such names, (the self) dwells in the beginningless and endless self, like great space within space.

[*Comment*: As the sacred text (Śruti) says, *sve mahimni pratiṣṭhitaḥ*, (he is) established in his own glory and power (*mahimni*) — *Chāndogya Upaniṣad* 7.24.1.]

12. In that clear (space-like self) this illusion of *saṁsāra* is seen like bangles and so forth in gold, like waves in water.

13. Fourteen categories of species of beings thrash[10] about enough in such a web[11] of *saṁsāra*, like birds (caught) in a net.

14. Among them, Yama, Candra, Sūrya, Indra[12] and the rest, their conduct as commanded, have reached the status of world-guardians over this *saṁsāra* of fivefold elements.

[*Comment*: Their conduct commanded as explained in the sacred texts and law books. Fivefold elements, the *tan-mātras*.[13]]

---

[10] Or, "flash about", as they come into being and disappear quickly in death.

[11] *Jāla*, the same word is used for both "web" and "net".

[12] There are eight regents of the cardinal points of the universe, starting from the east, and of those named here, Yama is the guardian of karam and death and therefore of the manes, the departed souls. He metes out the fruits of good and evil acts and rules over the inferno where evil beings suffer. Candra is the moon, Sūrya is the sun and Indra is the overlord of deities. In Hindu cosmology, these and other *deva*s are as much a part of the karmic cycle as the human mortals. Their elevated station is because of their karam.

[13] *Tan-mātra*s (the finer principles of the five gross elements) which are earth, water, fire, air and space. In Sāṅkhya philosophy, first the finer principles evolve, and then the gross elements.

15. "It is meritorious to follow this", to be followed, "It is sinful and is to be abandoned —" all this ruling has been established by them from the feelings[14] turned out from their own will.[15]

16. That (Yama's) mind up to this day, O sinless one, has remained set and steady in his own work, like a mountain[16] fallen in the flow (of the universal order).

17. When the period of four *yugas*[17] has passed some way, that Lord Yama, afraid of the sin arising from crushing the beings, undertakes (expiatory) ascetic vows.

18. Sometimes for eight years, or ten years, or twelve years, sometimes for five or seven years, and so forth, or sometimes even sixteen[18] years (he practises the vows).[19]

19. And while he thus remains as if indifferent (towards beings), undertaking the rules (of the observance), then death does not kill any beings (caught) in the net of the universe.

---

14 *Vedanā* (feeling or awareness). It is knowing, on the level of feeling.

15 *Saṅkalpa* (volition); the first movement of will to activate the grosser mind and senses, *saṅkalpa* also means "resolve".

16 The word used for mountain here is *acala* (unshakeable).

17 In the Indian system of cosmology, the universe is created and dissolved in regular and unending cycles. One such cycle is a *kalpa*, consisting of 8,640,000,000 years, divided into periods of creation and dissolution of equal duration. Each era of creation is further divided into fourteen (seven ascending, seven descending) Manu intervals, each ruled over by one law-giving Manu, collective or primal mind. Each of these *manvantaras* is divided into seventy-one cycles of four *yugas* each: Kṛta or Satya, Tretā, Dvāpara and Kali, in which virtue, harmony, and goodness prevail in respectively reduced strength.

18 In Hindu cosmology, one human year is one day and night of the *devas*. The count here is not in human terms.

19 There is no rule about duration of time in this.

20. Thereby the surface of the earth becomes so solidly packed with the crowds that (no-one) can pass through it; it becomes like a sweating elephant covered with mosquitoes in the rainy season.

21. O Rāma, the gods diminish these various beings by resorting to all different means in order to reduce the weight on the earth, O Rāma.

[*Comment*: The gods such as Viṣṇu take part-incarnations[20] and devise stratagems such as wars etc. to reduce the population.]

22. Thousands of *yuga*s and hundreds of (periods of such) procedures have thus passed, an unending number of beings and worlds.

[*Comment*: This burdening of the earth and the acts of incarnations has been repeated many times.]

23-24. Now, when some aeons (*yuga*s) will have passed, O good and holy (Rāma), this son of Vivasvat,[21] who is now Yama,

---

20 Cf. See *Bhagavad-Gītā* 4:7-8.

"Whenever there is the decline of virtue and the rise of evil, I create myself forth."

"To protect the good and to destroy the evil, to re-establish virtue, I am born from age to age."

When the Lord incarnates, many of his aspects, who are the deities, including the Feminine Power *śakti* as his would-be human female consort, also incarnate on earth to fulfil each his/her own assigned role in the drama of the Incarnate's humanized life. Even his "enemies" may be part-incarnations, playing their role in his mission of teaching, guiding and directing the destiny of a race or a chosen world. See also our translation of *Anu-Gītā*, to be published.

21 The current *manvantara* is called Vaivasvata because the present Manu is the mental son of Vivasvat, the Sun. It is only in the oral tradition of yoga initiations that the meaning of this aspect of the collective mind becomes clear and cannot be explained here.

the leader of the Manes, in order to overcome his own sin will undertake twelve years of the practice of observance in which he (will) desist from the destruction of people.

[*Comment*: The words of the stanza indicate that the observance consists of the practices leading from non-violence to the *nirvikalpa-samādhi*[22] that is the path of *rāja*-yoga.]

25. As a result, thereby this earth will become impassable (*nirandhra*[23]) because of the mortal beings who are not dying, who become a burden, and because of whom she is dejected, (like a forest) covered with (an unsurpassably thick net of vines).

26. With her limbs overcome with the weight, the earth will come to take refuge in Viṣṇu, like a charming, beloved woman, troubled and overcome by bandits, (running to) her husband.

27. Now, (then) Viṣṇu will descend to (or incarnate on) the earth with two bodies, together with parts of all the gods accompanying (these two incarnations) Nara and Nārāyaṇa.[24]

[*Comment*: Gods incarnate to follow Nara and Nārāyaṇa in order to help them in their acts.]

28. One of Viṣṇu's bodies will be the son of Vasudeva[25] (coming

---

[22] The eightfold path of yoga begins with five *yama*s (not to be confused with Yama the deity) of which the first is non-violence and the last is *nirvikalpa samādhi* (the purest state of consciousness, without any object).

[23] *Randhra* means a hole, *nirandhra*, so thick a crowd that there is no opening to pass through.

[24] *Nara* is man, Nārāyaṇa, is Viṣṇu, the all-preserving Spirit floating on waters. Cf. The Bible, Genesis 1:2.

[25] The name of Kṛṣṇa's physical father.

to be known) as Vāsudeva, and the second will be Arjuna, the son of Pāṇḍu.

29. A son of Dharma[26] will be born, known as Yudhiṣṭhira. That son of Pāṇḍu, knower of the law, (will be) a king of the earth girdled with the sea.[27]

30. His brother,[28] born of an uncle, will be known as Duryodhana. His very strong opponent will be Bhīma, like a mongoose to a snake.

31. As they become fiercely engaged in battle, snatching the (kingdom of) earth from each other, eighteen terrifying armies[29] will be participating.

32. By destroying them, Viṣṇu will reduce the weight on the earth with his Arjuna-personality carrying a great bow (named) Gāṇḍīva, O Rāma.

33. Viṣṇu's personality, assuming material form, in the name and so forth of Arjuna, will take on the nature of a man, endowed with pleasure and displeasure.[30]

---

[26] The five Pāṇḍava brothers, though sons of Pāṇḍu, were said to have been conceived from five deities. The eldest, Yudhiṣṭhira, was thus a son of Dharma (the deity known as) the Law itself. For this reason, Yudhiṣṭhira was absolutely virtuous, but for one or two failings.

[27] The mark of a *cakravartin* (an emperor of all earth), ruling over the entire *cakra* (circle) of the earth girdled with the sea.

[28] In India cousins are regarded as brothers and sisters; there is no word for "cousin".

[29] *Akṣauhiṇī*. One *akṣauhiṇī* consists of 21,870 chariots, as many elephant-riding soldiers, 65,610 cavalrymen and 109,350 of the infantry; a total of 2,18,700 soldiers. In the Mahābhārata War, eighteen *akṣauhiṇī*s participated, and all perished in eighteen days.

[30] There is a problem as to how human and how divine a God-incarnation is, and how much affected by human frailties, pains and pleasures. The answer is that it depends on how much of the divine nature has incarnated in a part-incarnation, or on how much of the human aspect needs to be exhibited for the particular role.

[*Comment*: Taking on human nature; that is, almost ignorant.]

34. Seeing his kinsmen in both armies ready to die, he will feel depressed and will cease to endeavour towards the battle.

35. O Rāma, in order to accomplish the single purpose at hand, Viṣṇu will enlighten that personality,[31] known as Arjuna, with his enlightened (*buddha*) personality (of Kṛṣṇa).

[*Comment*: The word *buddha* here means permanently self-enlightened (and not having to reach enlightenment through special effort). Nara and Nārāyaṇa are both divine incarnations. One playing ignorant and the other enlightened one guiding the ignorant. (The text now) elucidates the way the enlightenment was passed on.]

36. (The Self) is neither born, nor does it ever die; nor (once) having been does it cease to be. Unborn, permanent, eternal; this ancient One is not killed when the body is being killed.[32]

[*Comment*: After denying the first (i.e. birth) and the last (i.e. death) changes (*vikāras*[33] 27), now he proceeds to deny the possibilities of four changes that might occur in-between (birth and death); or (in the case of the enlightened) he negates the future birth, etc.]

37. He who thinks of this (self) as a killer, or knows him to be killed, both of them know not, for he is not a killer nor is he killed.[34]

---

31 *Deha*, literally "body".

32 *Bhagavad-Gītā* 2.20.

33 Matter undergoes *vikāras* (modifications) or changes of form which do not apply to the spirit.

34 *Bhagavad-Gītā* 2.19.

[*Comment*: Neither he who thinks of this self as a killer nor he who thinks of it as being killed, knows this self in its true nature. Ignorance alone is the cause of the illusion of being a killer or being the object of killing.]

38. Infinite, of one (unchanging) form, a being even finer, subtler, than space — what of this Self, (who is the) Supreme Lord, what, how, and by what can (anything) perish?

[*Comment*: What can be destroyed; in what manner; and for what cause? By using "what" in three modes, he suggests (a) perishable, (b) way of perishing, (c) cause and means of perishing.

39. Perceive the Self, infinite, unmanifest, without a beginning or middle, O you whose self is pure consciousness, whose body is pure consciousness; expansive (not delimited), in whom no blemish may be found. You are unborn, you are eternal, you are complete and free of all adversity.

[*Comment*: *Sphāra* (un-delimited); therefore one whom no blemish can touch. Your very nature and form is consciousness and for this reason you are unborn (and immortal). You are *nitya* (eternal) one who is devoid of ignorance and therefore of its result, the smear of any blemish. For this reason you can have no attachment to the kinmen, nor grief resulting from the thought of their death.]

In the Great Rāmāyaṇa of Vasiṣṭha, composed by Vālmīki as narrated by a messenger of *deva*s, the Path to Liberation, Nirvāṇa Section in the Narrative of Arjuna here ends of the fifty-second (52nd) chapter.

Chapter II

The Homily to Arjuna

(Now) is to be expounded: "relinquishing ego", marked first by renunciation of attachment; the natures of who is to be worshipped; what is to be known; (all) in order of differences of states.[1]

The Lord said:

1. You are not a slayer, Arjuna; abandon you this taint of false identification.[2] Free of decay and death, you yourself are the perennial Self (*ātman*).

   [*Comment*: "I am the killer of my kinsman" — this ego of I-ness (*ahantā-abhimāna*) and "These are my kinsmen" —

---

[1] This is the verse with which Ānanda-Bodhendra Sarasvati begins his commentary on the second chapter. "In order of difference of states"; that is to say the text explains how the *adhikārins* (people of different qualification), need to go through different levels of worship and knowledge. Those bound to the flesh need God Incarnate; those free of a limited personality go direct to *Brahman*, the non-qualitative Reality that transcends all limitation.

[2] *Abhimāna*: that function of ego (*ahaṅkāra*) whereby the conscious self assumes an identity with an object to which it (the self) lends its consciousness. By this process the true consciousness, life and power of the self are observed. Thus the self, dwelling in the human body, falsely knows itself to be limited to the time, space, sequence, and experience of that human personality and the self in a tree's body stands mute, with most of its will inactive. Similarly a person takes on the *abhimāna* of being rich or poor; being a Chinese, American or Indian; being a Catholic or Jew; being male or female, having a name and form. Thus he assumes a friendship or enmity and "murders" an "enemy" to benefit a "friend".

this ego of mine-ness (*mamatā-abhimāna*)[3] — this is the cause of all your sorrow. So he begins by saying: "O Arjuna, free of the six waves of old age, death[4] and so forth, therefore eternal, you are yourself the Self of all beings, including your kinsmen. Therefore you cannot be anyone's slayer." The next verse describes the result of such a realization.]

2. One who has no thought associated with I, whose faculty of discrimination (*buddhi*) is not smeared, even upon slaying these people, neither kills nor becomes bound.

   [*Comment*: When undertaking a duty such as killing (in battle) a person who does not have the thought "I am killing", and whose *buddhi*, following the act, is not smeared with the consequent pleasure or depression and so forth, such a person does not kill, even when separating the lives of others from their bodies. Since the eternal, essential One cannot be touched by modifications and changes such as death, and since the body and so forth are mere *māyā*, their slaying is unreal, like the existence of the son of a barren woman. Therefore, like God, he is not bound by the results of a presumed sin arising from such (thought).]

3. Whatever (false) perception arises is experienced within; "This is that", "I am that", "That is mine", — abandon such internal perceptions.

   [*Comment*: It is only the movement of the body and so on that slays. When one has the illusion of identity with that

---

[3] The *abhimāna* develops in two stages: *aham* and *mama* (ego and meum, I and mine). First there is the assumption of a false identity and then, naturally, one enters into the resulting relationships, possessing and being possessed. If I am a tree, naturally the branches, twigs and roots are mine, and I fight for the ground I need for my roots. Once *aham* (ego) "I" is abandoned, the *mama* (meum, "mine") naturally vanishes.

[4] Sorrow, delusion, hunger, thirst, decay, death. See also footnote on verse 64, for six *bhāva-vikāra*s.

body, then the nature of being a slayer and so one, which belongs to the body, reflects on the self. Therefore, give up that perception of false identity. This false awareness consists of the identification with the body, etc. imposed on the Self, which is within the heart, or the opposite of the identity you know. Give up this erroneous attitude that "I am the aggregate of cause and effect", "I am that slayer", "I have connection with this body and so forth", "these kinsmen, etc. are mine".

4. "I am united"; "I perish"; you suffer so only because of this (error), all around helpless with pain and pleasure, O Bhārata.

   [*Comment*: Through the above internal perception, "I am joined to the attributes such as being a slayer"; "destroyed because of the sins accruing from such union"; "I am joined to the undesirable experiences of this world such as the loss of kinsmen and the undesirable results of the other world such as falling into Hell" — because of this false awareness you suffer from pains and pleasures.

5. Because of actions being performed by the *guṇas*,[5] each according to its share, which (act as) parts of one's own Self, with self deluded by ego, one thinks, "I am the doer".

   [*Comment*: The actions (are) being performed by the body and senses etc., which are a modification of the *guṇa*s such as *sattva*, and which are parts of the self only in so far as they cause an assumption of delimitations of the (delimited) self.

6. Let the eye see, let the ear hear, let the skin touch "this" (whatever); let the tongue go towards taste. Who am I in all this? What is the propriety (of such a question)?

---

[5] See footnote on I.1 and footnote on verse 22 of this chapter. For *guṇa*s, see *BhG* chapters 14, 17, 18.

[*Comment*: In *vimarśa*, the highest self-contemplation, only the senses like the eyes etc. are engaged in their subjects like form. It is not an engagement of *ātman* (the self). So, there is no possibility of *ātman* claiming the acts of these senses as his own. Even the question, "Who am I in all this activity of the senses?" is inappropriate.]

7. Even when the mind of the great Self, you, is absorbed in the activity of calculating[6] (and wishing), (when you know that) "I am nothing as to this matter" what part of you can then share any suffering (*kleśa*[7])?

   [*Comment*: This *kalanā* is (*saṅkalpa*) resolve, intention, etc. Though the aggregate of the inner sense, such as the mind, may remain absorbed in its own actions of wishing and assuming (*saṅkalpa*), when you see that none of these is I, then what part of you can have any share of *kleśa* because of which you may grieve?]

8. O Bhārata, that what has been produced by many (constituents), through (their) aggregation, are mistaken as one through painful false identification (*abhimāna*). This can only lead one to ridicule.

   [*Comment*: (The various aspects of personality are composed) as a result of the aggregation and application

---

6 From verb root *kal*, to calculate (the way mind keeps calculating so many options), count, to be temporal. The same root is the source of *kāla* (time) and *kalā*, a digit, component part, phase, like *kalā*s of the moon. Also cognate to "calculate" and "calendar".

7 *Kleśa*: According to the *Yoga-Sūtras* of Patañjali (II.3), there are five *kleśa*s, namely: (i) ignorance of the true self resulting in, (ii) I-am-ness, (iii) attraction, (iv) aversion, and (v) an inhibition against death. These cause the waves and operations of the mind to be sullied (*kliṣṭa*). The verb root *kliṣ* means both "sully" or "strain" and "cause pain" or "suffer". In Yoga psychology the two are one and the same. Only an impure mind suffers; painful thoughts are an impurity to be bleached off the mind.

of multiple factors. Not a single one of those factors should really share the suffering of the total aggregate. The self is totally beyond and out of this aggregate; how can it suffer the discomforts of that aggregate, which is external to it?]

9. With the body, with the mind, with the faculty of discrimination (*buddhi*), and even with the senses alone, the *yogī*s perform their actions (only) when they have given up attachment (and only) in order to purify themselves.

[*Comment*: A person who is free of ego and of attachment to the fruits of his actions, his threefold action with the body, speech and mind performed in accordance with the ordinance of scriptures, has only one purpose, the Supreme Realization, through the awakening of knowledge by means of the purification of mind. (This includes such acts as fighting in battle, enjoined on a kṣatriya.) Then how can you feel any suffering from your *dharma* (your duty to fight)? The *yogī*s in this verse are those aspiring to rise. "*Yogī*s" here means those desirous of rising, seekers of liberation.]

10. Those whose personality is not directed towards death through the poison-powder of I-ness, free of all (such) disease, perform nothing, gather nothing, even when performing actions and gathering their fruits.

[*Comment*: Directed towards death means leading to repeated cycles of death, which is caused by excessive running after physical pleasures. Free of disease, i.e. free of stains such as attractions and aversions. They may be performing worldly (*laukika*) or scripture-ordained sacraments (*śāstrīya*) actions, and experiencing the incidental fruits that accrue because of their natural association with actions (*ānuṣaṅgika*).]

11. Sullied with the foulness of "mine-ness" this personality cannot at all shine (as beautiful) when a man, however

wise, knowing however much, (behaves) like a man of poor conduct.

[*Comment*: "Does not shine"[8] means "is unfit for correct worldly or spiritual conduct".]

12. Whoever is free of "mine-ness" and is without "I-ness", alike in pain and pleasure, and forgiving, he is not smeared, even doing the enjoined and un-enjoined (acts).

[*Comment*: Right (*kāryam*) and wrong (*akāryam*): duties that must be done, as enjoined by the scripture, and those that need not be done, such as secular acts, not prohibited actions as that is not applicable (here).]

13. And, O Son of Pāṇḍu, this your own highest duty, enjoined for a kṣatriya, even though (appearing) cruel, is the highest goal leading both to happiness and elevation.

[*Comment*: Your duty in the battle, even though appearing cruel is (ultimately) conducive to happiness, such as knowledge of *Brahman* through the purification of mind, and elevation, such as fulfilment of duty, reputation, gaining of kingdom, heaven and so forth.]

14. Even if (normally) censured, even if strange,[9] even if of the order of *adharma*, since your own duty is the best, so (by doing it), receive immortality here.

[*Comment*: "Besides killing the kinsmen a censurable act of killing the revered elders — how am I to do that", in this doubt, (Kṛṣṇa) imparts a hope based on an oath of truth.[10]

---

[8] In Sanskrit language, verbs meaning "shine" (*rāj, bhā, śubh*) often express the idea "looking beautiful", because light is beauty.

[9] *Anyat* means "other". Here we have translated it as "strange".

[10] *Satya-śapatha*: Somewhat equivalent to Pāli *saccha-kiriya*, where one resorts to some statement of truth by the power of which one may undertake what may otherwise appear untenable or impossible. Here the power of truth lies in the fact that the acts that Arjuna is embarking on are enjoined by the scripture.

Here, in this battle, so long as the action is truthful (*satya*), that is in accordance with scriptural injunctions, it will take you to immortality in the sense of gaining victory.]

15. One's own duty leads even a fool to the highest good (*śreyas*); how much more so for one of pure wisdom? An intellect with a diminishing ego, even fallen, is not smeared.

16. O Dhanañjaya, give up attachment, perform your actions dwelling in yoga. When you are free of attachment, performing actions as they arise, you (will) not be bound.

[*Comment*: Sins arise from greed and disease from (the body's) juices. In accordance with this maxim there arises the possibility of a transgression of *dharma* (for a kṣatriya) if the battle is undertaken out of greed for an expansion of the kingdom. However, that possibility is avoided if, by abandoning attachment to results (fruits of actions), one abides in yoga, which is defined as evenness in accomplishment or failure because one whose intelligence is unsmeared by ego (false I-ness) is not brought to bondage even by most heinous of sins.[11] (Kr̥ṣṇa) teaches (here) that abiding in yoga.

17. Your body becoming as of the tranquil *Brahman*, perform *Brahman*-absorbed action. Thus, with all your conduct, surrender to *Brahman*. You (will) become that very *Brahman* within a moment.

18. All your purposes surrendered to[12] God, God your self, free of corruption,[13] Become the very God who is the Self

---

11 *Mahāpātakas*: These are normally five but the number and the lists vary from text to text. These include: (1) killing a person of priest-philosopher caste (*brahma-hatyā*) and (2) drinking alcohol.

12 *Brahman* in stanza 17; here *Īśvara*, the Ruling One, personal God.

13 *Nirāmaya*: Throughout this text, *āmaya* means spiritual or psychological disease. In non-metaphysical Sanskrit it often denotes physical disease.

of all beings, and be (thus) an adornment to the earth.

[*Comment*: The action, as being recommended below, being performed with the awareness of surrender to God, will not lead to your bondage. If you cannot reach the transcendental, non-qualitative *Brahman*, then perform your actions with the thought of surrender to the personal God (*Īśvara*). Thereby, too, there will not accrue a bondage to karam.]

19. Renouncing all resolves (*saṅkalpa*[14]), even, serene of mind, a meditative sage, performing actions with (your) self harmonized in the yoga of renunciation, liberate your mentative faculty.[15]

[*Comment*: Or, another way you would not be bound by actions is by the stratagem of *saṁnyāsa-yoga* (yoga of renunciation) defined as abandoning all intention (*saṅkalpa*).]

Arjuna said:

20. Lord, of abandoning attachment as well as of surrender to *Brahman*, and of complete[16] renunciation comprising surrender to God,

21. And, (my) Lord, between knowledge and yoga, what is the

---

[14] *Saṅkalpa*: The word *saṅkalpa* occurs repeatedly in the text. When self takes on an *abhimāna*, its will initiates thought-processes that concern identities and their consequent relationships and possessions. These processes, resolves, wishes, fancies, are all included in the word *saṅkalpa*. It is through *saṅkalpa* that God becomes or creates the universe and through *saṅkalpa* alone that a person draws to himself his environment and circumstance. *Saṅkalpa* is the creative (and destructive) will of the conscious (universal or individual) self going out into the material world by way of thought processes.

[15] *Mati*: way of thinking, opining; instrument of thought, the mind.

[16] ...s [renunciation], in every way.

division?[17] Do tell me this, in sequence, in order to turn off the great delusion.

[*Comment*: Thus taught, Arjuna, desirous of knowing the division of the renunciation of attachment and so forth, by their definitions, asks (the questions posed in the verses).]

The Lord said:

22. Upon all thought-processes becoming tranquil,[18] when (even the most) solid propensities[19] have been dissolved[20] and nothing remains in the form of fancy,[21] what is (experienced) (the wise) know as the Supreme *Brahman*.

[*Comment*: Because the total abandonment of attachment is not possible without the thorough realization of the Essence, the Lord first teaches the Essence of the *Brahman*-Self. *Brahman* is the same as the inward self without the *prapañca*, the network of relative existence and experience;

---

[17] *Vibhāga* (division into categories).

[18] *Saṁśānta, śānti* means not just a state of tranquillity in this case but total cessation, gradual tranquillity, and coming down to a point where the thought processes and the propensities disappear.

[19] *Vāsanā*. The next stage after *saṅkalpa*, whereby momentum is created, propelling the creative/destructive urge in a certain direction.

[20] *Praśānta*, as *saṁśānta*.

[21] *Bhāvanā*: According to the philosophy of *Yoga-Vāsiṣṭha*, the processes of karam pass through four stages: (i) *vedanā*, the first experience; (ii) *bhāvanā*, contemplating the experience, thus strengthening its memory and psychological impact; (iii) *vāsanā*, when a certain experience, memory and tendency thus strengthened goes deep into *citta* and into the *karmāśaya* (the storehouse of karam), to such a point that it becomes the origin of further inclinations and tendencies (here translated as propensities), so that personality develops a momentum in a certain direction; (iv) *kalanā*, the final gathering of the sum total of a lifetime's actions, which goes with the subtle body and determines the state and nature of the experiences of the next incarnation.

it is found only in the experience of the realization of the maturity of *nirvikalpa samādhi*.]

23. Those who have cultivated their faculty of discrimination (*buddhi*) know that endeavour to be knowledge (*jñāna*) and yoga. "The entire universe and I are *Brahman*." This they know to be the surrender to *Brahman*.

[*Comment*: Endeavour towards that (is divided into knowledge (*jñāna*) and yoga). Knowledge is when the operations of the mind (*vṛttis*) are concentrated on the nature of that (*Brahman*) and this *vṛtti* is bearing the fruit of turning off the ignorance. Yoga is when the *vṛtti* is flowing like an unbroken stream in accord with and in that direction (*anukūla*, not against the stream). The surrender to *Brahman* is chiefly warding off the ego (*ahaṅkāra*, I-maker), which establishes the false feeling of identity. (A consciousness opposite to) and warding off the empirical existence which should be thought of as identical to *Brahman* and (warding off) the *ahaṅkāra* which establishes the false identity with the empirical existence of the world — this is the surrender to *Brahman*.]

24. Void within, void without, like the heart of a stone,[22] pacific, clear like a sheath and encasement of space, neither an object of perception nor beyond the perceiver.[23]

[*Comment*: The nature of *Brahman* is described in this stanza: that the world and the ego are superimposed on *Brahman* and that this superimposition is to be warded off. If the (existence) of all objects of perception is denied,

---

22 Just as a stone inside and outside is the same.

23 Compare *Yoga-Sūtras* of Patañjali (II.6, 17, 20, 23). The objects of the world and of ego are perceived but the Self is pure *dṛś*, the consciousness principle. The Supreme One is not beyond the consciousness principle but is that principle itself. See our commentary on *dṛśi-śakti* in *Yoga-Sūtras*, available from ahymsinpublishers@gmail.com

then is not the perceiver also denied, since that perceiver too is perceived? The answer is given that the perceiver's perceivability would be denied only if there were another perceiver to perceive the original perceiver, but this is not the case.]

25. Just a little[24] arising from that, just a little occurrence as "other", that (very mild) appearance of the universe like (a reflection in the) sky; voidness.

[*Comment*: Just a mild appearance as "other" from that *Brahman* is the appearance of empirical reality; like a city of *gandharvas*[25] in the sky; this too is mere void.]

26. Somewhat of a feeling of "I" arising from the consciousness with reference to each individual being, counted as a ten-millionth[26] of the ten-millionth part (of consciousness), what is there to grasp or insist on?

[*Comment*: In order to express the desirability of renunciation he says that the superimposition of "I" in each individual among the *jīvas*, who are the parts of that

---

[24] *Īṣat* (just a little). Just a slight tension in the trough begins the rise of a wave and the existence of space is so slight as to be almost unnoticeable, yet it is the substratum of all movement, time, and sequence of the universe. A *yogī* of acute perception does not look at the gross movement but at the very finest, first vibration, while it is still almost non-existent. Thus he observes one becoming/creating the "other". When he traces the sequence back, he dissolves it all: the "other" ceases, and the *yogī* is the *Brahman*.

[25] *Gandharva*: a species of celestial beings who, in *Mahābhārata* and the Purāṇas are often depicted as visiting the earth and interacting with mortals. Illusions of cities appearing on the horizon, as through a mirage, may be the work of *gandharvas*, but only in legend and mythology; upon close examination no such city of the sky can be found.

[26] *Koṭi*, Sanskrit for ten million, often used simply for high numbers.

Brahman, is just like the superimposition of an empirical world on that *Brahman*; therefore any insistence on this "I" is inappropriate.]

27. This undifferentiated one alone has become, as it were, differentiated. Even bounded by separateness one does not think "I am not".

[*Comment*: "This I am", this thought, is not separable from one's own base of (transcendental) consciousness because the delimitation leading to separateness is not (possible) in *Brahman*. As "no-one" is non-existent, "no-one" can comprehend "I am not". If separateness is to be proved by the reason of apprehension and, alternatively, apprehension through separateness, then the argument is fallacious and one of the two stands will have to be abandoned. Therefore it is better to abandon the concept of separateness itself.]

28. Just as I am here, so also is the jar and so on, or a monkey also. Similarly, the ocean (has) its own self-being; therefore what is this grasping towards I-ness?

[*Comment*: What has been said about "I-ness" should be applied also to the mental endeavour that goes into establishing the "meum" about a jar and so forth. Expressing this, he strengthens the renunciation of the very "I-ness" (from which the meum arises). Just as (within oneself) the endeavour of "I-ness" is not separable and divisible, so also, in reverse (in the outside world), the I-ness of me or of a jar or of a monkey is inseparable. The endeavour of both kinds (ego and meum) is only the full ocean that is oneself, *ātman* the self. The prejudice in grasping (*āgraha*) of (the little) "I-ness" (*ahantā-graha*)[27] is untenable and inappropriate.]

---

[27] Here we have translated *ahnatāgraha* in two ways: *ahantā-āgraha* and *ahantā-graha* and integrated the two meanings.

29. Even though the differences of qualitative thought (*vikalpa*) flash in the self, who is the very essence of awareness, even though variegated with a variety of pictures (there remains the fundamental) oneness. Why is this very oneness not grasped?

[*Comment*: Even though there appear the differences of all the qualitative thoughts such as "I" and "mine-ness", variegated with the various pictures of the different objects of this (each subjective) "I", the fundamental of the flashing of their existence, accompanied with three states (wakefulness, dream, and sleep), whose nature is only the essence of pure awareness, and who is the witness of all the coming and going of the qualitative thoughts, this one, inward self remains only one. This being the case, why do we not insist on that one (I)?]

30. When one knows these categories (and) then the loss of that (I and mine-ness in his) *buddhi*, (and the resulting) relinquishing of the fruit of action, that (is what) the wise call renunciation.

[*Comment*: Contemplating the above categories, when a person has understood the essential and the non-essential, then in his intellect there is loss of the insistence on "I" and "mine", which means that it naturally results in his relinquishing the attachment to the fruits of all actions. That is true renunciation.]

31. Relinquishing the nets of all mental resolve (*saṅkalpa*) is called non-attachment; contemplating that the entire network of experience and feelings (*kalanā*) is the contemplation (*bhāvanā*) that it is all One Godhood.

32. This alone is surrender to God, when the appearance of duality has vanished. In the consciousness-self the differentiation of these exists only through name, by virtue of ignorance.

[*Comment*: (Of the four questions asked in verses 20-21, the second and third questions are answered here), which implies an answer to the first: that non-attachment means relinquishing all mental resolve. The fourth question is answered: contemplate all nets of duality to be the same as God (who is) their source cause (*upādāna*),[28] as stated in the text (Śruti), "initiative of speech" (*Chāndogya Upaniṣad* 6.1.4).]

33. "Awareness-as-self" (*bodhātman*) is indeed the meaning of (all) words; the universe is one, there is no doubt about it. I am the expectations, I the universe, I the reflexive self,[29] I too the action.

[*Comment*: To affirm the same as above, the Lord states his *vibhūti*, variant of his power, namely, being the self of all. *Jagat*, the moving world; *svam*, the substratum of actions.]

34. I am time, I am non-dual, I am the dual, I also am the universe. Let your mind be fixed on me, my devotee,

---

[28] *Upādāna*. In logic, *upādāna* is normally the material cause. Since *Brahman* is not of matter, the word has to be translated as "origin" in a general sense. In strictly formal Vedānta philosophy, the universe is not a transmutation of *Brahman* in the same sense in which a jar is of clay, or the sense in which the dualistic Sāṅkhya philosophy proposes the universe to be a modification (*vikāra*) of matter. To translate *upādāna* here as "the material out of which anything is made" (Apte's *Sanskrit–English Dictionary*) would defeat the very argument of the chapter.

Chāndogya Upaniṣad (Śvetaketu narrative) VI.1.4-6: "It is dear, as by (understanding) a single lump of clay everything that is of clay may be understood as a transmutation is only an upholding of words, a name. 'Clay' alone, however, is the truth." And so about the nuggets of gold and iron.

[29] *Svam*, the personality, a possession of the true self. The word is often used in a reflexive–possessive sense, as *svo dehaḥ* (own body), *svam riktham* (own wealth). Whatever is my own, *svam*, that I the self am, therefore what can be "mine"?

worshipping me, bow to Me. Thus uniting the Self in yoga, intent upon Me, you will come only to Me.

[*Comment*: The non-dual transcendental and the dual lower nature and the world controlled by that (lower nature[30]), I am all those. This means that your mind should be fixed on one of these two forms, according to your preparedness (*adhikāra*). "Devoted to Me" means that you should be filled with the feelings and expressions of nine kinds of *bhakti* in the form of hearing and singing of Me, worshipping Me either with the worship of knowledge or worship in (ritual) acts. In this above-mentioned way of two kinds uniting yourself (in yoga), that is, entering your mind-field (*citta*) into me, you will come and find me as the self of your own self. This you will find in the sequence of direct experience (*sākṣāt*).]

Arjuna said:

35. O Lord of gods, you have two forms; (the transcendental) beyond and the immanent lower (in this world). What (is) the form, of what nature, and when should I resort to and abide in it for fulfilment (*siddhi*)?[31]

[*Comment*: Following the instruction concerning the two natures (of God) in verse 34, Arjuna now asks how to know the qualification (*adhikāra*) and the appropriate time for (worshipping either of the two natures).]

---

30 The word *rūpam* (form) is used. We avoid translating it as "form" with reference to the formless *Brahman*. Why is the word *rūpam* used? It is to indicate the very being, and not a supposed qualitative description of *Brahman*, which is primarily non-qualitative and beyond description.

31 The symbols Viṣṇu the Preserver holds in his four hands. These symbolic or incarnate appearances are for those whose minds cannot grasp pure *Brahman*. For meanings of the symbols read Alain Danielou, *Hindu Polytheism*, Pantheon Books, Random House, New York, 1964.

The Lord said:

36. O Sinless One, know My two forms; the common one and the transcendental. The common form is endowed with hands and so forth, holding conch, discus and mace.

[*Comment*: Common: easily understandable for ordinary people.]

37. That which is my transcendental form has no beginning and end; it is one, without corruption,[32] and it is expressed by words such as *Brahman*, "Self", "Supreme Self".

[*Comment*: The Supreme Form, difficult to attain by those of impure mind.]

38. Until you are fully awakened and remain without the knowledge of Self, be intent upon the worship of the god with the four-armed form.[33]

39. When in due order you become enlightened, you will know that nature beyond; the form of Me that has no beginning and no end, and by (knowing which) one is not born again.[34]

[*Comment*: "In due order" means "with the gradual purification of mind".]

40. If, however, your being has known (the aspect of mine) that is worthy of knowledge, O destroyer of enemies, then resort immediately to my Self, the Self of (your) self.[35]

---

32 *Āmaya*: corruption, disease or illness, whether physical or mental.

33 Viṣṇu.

34 One is freed from the cycles of re-incarnation. On the other hand, those whose objects of devotion are symbolic or "God become flesh" forms of God, being attached to flesh, keep returning to the worlds of flesh. Even the heavenly world is a world, not liberation.

35 To my *ātman* and to the *ātman* of (your own) *ātman*.

[*Comment*: I have told you of devotion to the qualitative (*saguṇa*) nature, considering the possibility of a lack of purity of (your) mind. If, however, your being (*bhāva*), that is, mind, is so pure (as to be one with) *Brahman*, whose nature is totality of cognition (*vijñāna-eka-svabhāva*), and who is worthy of being known, you should resort to the indivisible and completely perfect Self. (This you may do) by coalescing My Self, (who am) God and your Self; (My Self) in its transcendental nature determining its objects, and your self in its objective nature determining its essence.[36] This coalescence is between investigating the meaning of the word *tat* (that),[37] which is Myself, and investigating the meaning of the word *tvam* (thou), which is yourself. Then resort to the indivisible completely Full Self. Awakening to this, then, be firmly established in it. "Resort to", that is, becoming enlightened: be resolute upon it.]

41. As I teach you, "I am this" and "I am this", I am expounding to you this truth of (your own) self.

[*Comment*: The purpose of the declarations of glory that "I am the hopes", "I am the universe", (in verses such as 36-37) and so forth is to contemplate and determine the true (God) nature of the substratum of each of these as your own reality (*sva-tattva-pariśodhana*).]

42. I believe you are well enlightened; you have come to rest at the (highest) pedestal;[38] you are liberated from thought

---

36 Literally *tat-tvam* (that-ness); the essence or essential nature, the very *ens* of an entity.

37 In the *mahā-vākya, tat tvam asi* (that thou art), the great sentence from the Upaniṣad that is assigned to a Vedānta initiate to contemplate, analyse and absorb.

38 *Pada*, here meaning the highest state aimed at.

processes. Let (yourself) be the true one self.[39]

[*Comment*: In order to encourage (Arjuna), (Kṛṣṇa) addresses him as if he is already an accomplished one (*siddha*) (but what he really means is) "When you understand my teachings, you will soon come to rest in your real nature."]

43. Your self harmonized in yoga,[40] holding an even view towards all, see the self dwelling in all beings and all beings in the self.

[*Comment*: Understanding the self as the substratum, the beings superimposed upon it.[41]]

44. He devotes (himself) to the self dwelling in all beings (and as such) oneness of the self; operating in every way, yet he is not born again.

[*Comment*: "Operating in all different ways" means whether remaining in *samādhi* or functioning in the practical world.

45. "Unity" is the meaning of the word "all" and "the self" is the meaning of the word "one". For one who has found the self (to be) neither existent nor non-existent, that is his immediately.

[*Comment*: In this verse he expounds the meaning of the verse 44. One sees the Self as the substratum in all beings, and then he himself becomes the significatum of the word "all". Finding nothing else separates from that substratum,

---

39 *Satya-eka-ātmamaya*, literally "truth-one-self-comprising" is difficult to translate in coherent English. Be what you truly are, one truth, the self; one self the true reality; self that is the one true reality; self that is One and the true reality.

40 *Yoga-yukta-ātmā*: the yoga-yoked self; the self united with *Brahman* in yoga.

41 *Adhyasta*: *adhyāsa* is the Vedānta theory of superimposition, such as water superimposed on a mirage, silver on a glinting sea-shell, the empirical universe on pure self.

he finds the oneness. Now, the meaning of the word "one" is that the self,[42] remaining in the nature of the inward self, is neither existent in the sense of being divided in the threefold world of forms, nor is he non-existent, i.e. having the nature of the dual subtle elements but that it has the nature of one expansive bliss and consciousness. When this self comes within the experience of one, then he immediately attains the absoluteness (*kaivalya*) of expansiveness and bliss, devoid of all birth and other modifications and changes. As soon as this one of the singular nature of plenitude (*bhūmā*) and bliss comes within one's experience, then immediately, simultaneous with such experience, the isolation-liberation (*kaivalya*) is effected that is of the same nature of plenitude and bliss, free of all corruption and modification such as (re-)birth.]

46. That illuminator, who is the illumination inside the minds of the threefold world, "I am the self". Coming to that maturity is the (ultimate) determination.

[*Comment*: This statement is meant to answer the possible allegation that the self is too far beyond us, since no one can experience it.]

47. The experience of flavour, that is found in all the waters of all the three worlds, sweetness in the products (of milk from the) cows and (salt in the waters) of the sea; all this flavour is this very self, O Bhārata.

[*Comment*: This too is to prove that the experience of *rasa* (flavour, taste, joy) of self is not beyond our experience.]

48. The subtle experience[43] that remains inside all beings, free

---

[42] That = Self, *Brahman*.

[43] *Anubhava*, experience; *anu* (after), *bhava* (being, happening). What remains (in the mind) after something has happened.

from the objects of experience, is this self, permeating all.

[*Comment*: Subtle, because it is not noticed in the absence of the objects of experience.]

49. As butter[44] remains inside all milk, so the Supreme One remains in the bodies of all objects.

[*Comment*: Inside all objects as their substratum; inside all bodies as their illuminator.]

50. As Light[45] (is) both inside and outside all the jewels of the sea, so am I (inside and outside) all personalities,[46] remaining as if not at all there.

[*Comment*: Just as the light inside all jewels also shines outside them, in the same manner.]

51. Just as space (exists) both inside and outside a thousand jars, so do I remain the self (inside and out) of the bodies of the three worlds.

[*Comment*: This verse provides another analogy for the self being unsmeared, as indicated by "as if not at all there" (verse 50).]

52. As the form of a string, threaded through hundreds of pearls (remains hidden while joining them), so this self remains unnoticed in a hundred thousand personalities.[47]

[*Comment*: It permeates within and holds them together.]

53. In the entire cloud of objects from Brahmā to a blade of grass this common principle, existence, (the wise) know as the unborn (eternal) self.

---

44 *Ghṛtam* (ghee, clarified butter).

45 *Tejas* (brilliance; the fire principle).

46 *Deha*, literally "body", since body is often mistaken to be the whole personality.

47 *Deha*.

[*Comment*: This state, remaining unmodified as the substratum, self, in those (objects) is the state of being *Brahman*, and that alone is real. The analogies above of the thread through the pearls as all-pervading, or the light in the gems as manifest *jīva* are both superimposed and dependent, established only for the empirical operation of the world and not real. He says this verse in order to refute the existence (of differentiations such as) the slayer and the slain, the sin from such acts, and someone who brings forth the result of such acts, as someone different from one's own self.]

54. That *Brahman* remains just *Brahman*, even though a form flashes just a little as "I-am-ness" and so forth, the worldness and so forth, in an order (of karam, causations and operations) causing illusion.

55. This self alone takes on the form of the world; what here is killed, what kills? What in it, O Arjuna, is smeared with the grief of the world, good or bad?

[*Comment*: Just another analogy to illustrate not being smeared with transgressions such as slaying and so forth, which are all superimposed on *Brahman*.]

56. Like a mirror with relation to reflections, remaining like a witness, not perishing in things that perish; he alone sees who sees this.

57. "I am this, I am not this", is what I say. Thus I am the self, all-self and self of all;[48] know me thus, O Pāṇḍava.

[*Comment*: In all bodies (the sense) "I", "I", such ever expanding part of consciousness (*cid-aṁśa*) — that is what I verily am is. In all personalities extended as I, this particle of consciousness I alone am; I am not a part of the objects,

48 *Sarvātman* may be translated as all-self or self of all; all this is self, self that is all.

senses and bodies, which are unconscious (*jaḍa*). Thus even a statement concerning the differentiations of "I" is like the differentiation between the mirror and the reflection in it, which is not the mirror, or like the reflections in many mirrors. Just as a mirror does not affect (literally "smear") the object being reflected, so also I too am the non-dual all-self.]

58. All these modifications of creations and dissolutions function only dwelling in the *citta* (collective mind), in the (false) "I-ness" (ego) in the self, like waves of water in the sea.

[*Comment*: In the *citta* which has the *vr̥tti* of *abhimāna* (false identification) known as *aham̐-tā* (false I-ness).

59. There is the stone-nature of mountains, wood-nature of trees, and water-nature of waves;[49] just so is the selfness of all objects.

[*Comment*: Selfness is the transcendental reality.]

60. He who sees the self dwelling in all beings and all beings in the self, he, in that way, sees the self as not a doer.

[*Comment*: "Not a doer". Just as a mirror does nothing when a reflection (mimics) the movement (of a reflected object).]

61. Just as it is (the same) water in the waves of many forms and changes; just as gold (in many forms) bangles and so forth, so is the self in all beings, O Arjuna.

62. Just as the various multitudes of waves all roll in the water and bangles and so forth (exist) in gold, so do beings (exist) in the higher self.

63. All the various objects, beings, and the great *Brahman*,

---

[49] Literally, stoneness, woodness, and waterness of stone, wood and water.

O Bhārata, know to be all one; there is not the slightest separateness.

[*Comment*: Again, like the mirror and the reflection in it.]

64. In all the three worlds, what is there that can be subject to (*gamya*) the modifications of being (*bhāva-vikāra*)?[50] What is there that is yours, what of the world (truly exists)? Why are you confused for nothing?[51]

[*Comment*: When the unmodified *Brahman* is all one, and the only one, what is there, other than this, that is subject to the modifications of being such as birth and so on? Then how can there be modifications of being, such as slaying of kinsmen, and is there some world other than the self? None.]

65. Hearing it thus and very definitely effecting "no-fear"[52]

---

[50] There are six *bhāva-vikāras*, modifications, transmutations, changes in state, expressed by the verb "be". These are: *jāyate* (it was not there in that form and now) is born; *asti* (now) is; *vipariṇamate*, immediately upon coming into being, begins to) undergo change; *vardhate* (first it) grows; *apakṣīyate*, then diminishes; and finally *vinaśyati*, it disappears, changes its appearance, becomes something else, and starts on the sixfold modification over again. All verbs are said to be expressive of some variety of one of these states of "be". This would apply to fighting and slaying also. One who is in *Brahman* is in the absolute "Be", without these verb modifications.

[51] *Mudhā*, in vain, to no end, no aim, to no gain.

[52] *Abhayam*, no subjective fear, no objective danger. Since fear in the mind attracts or generates dangerous situations that in turn reinforce fear, the same one word is used to express both the subjective and objective ends of the particular experience. One of the vows of *saṁnyāsa*, the renunciation ceremony of the swami monastic order, is *abhayam sarva-bhūtebhyo mattaḥ*, which may be translated "Let no beings fear me, let me present no danger to any being". Since fear/danger arises from "another", where there is no "other", but all one *Brahman* self, there is no fear/danger.

within, the *jīvan-muktas* (liberated living ones)[53] wander in this world; the saints, whose inner being is even-flowing.[54]

[*Comment*: They contemplate within themselves *Brahman* as *abhaya* (i.e. upon knowing which, no fear/danger exists).]

66. Free of pride and delusion, having conquered the faults that arise from attachment and company,[55] concerned ever with spiritual self alone, their desires all having turned off, free from dichotomies (like) the awareness of pains and pleasures, no longer deluded, they go to that immutable state.

[*Comment*: They can attain also *videha* absoluteness.[56]]

In the Great Rāmāyaṇa of Vasiṣṭha, composed by Vālmīki as narrated by a messenger of *devas*, the Path to Liberation, Nirvāṇa Section in the Narrative of Arjuna here ends of the fifty-third (53rd) chapter.

---

53 *Santaḥ*, plural of continuous participle of the verb root *as*, "to be". Those who are only in "Be", just Being, not going through the six modes, nor "doing".

54 *Āśaya*, the inner personality. *Sama-rasa-āśaya*, whose inner personality (*āśaya*) has attained an even flow rather than being subject to excitations and depressions or, deeper still, the coalescence of their very essence as described in verse 40 above.

55 *Saṅga* means both keeping company and attachment.

56 This is not the same as the *videha-samādhi* of the *laya-yogins*, followers of the yoga of dissolution, which is described in the *Yoga-Sūtras* of Patañjali (I.19). There, it is a state of dissolving matter and material awarenss to a fine degree, reaching a material void, and mistaking it for all-consciousness. Here, as in the tradition of the Upaniṣads, *videha* (the bodiless one) is a term of compliment, and denotes one who remains dwelling in the body yet is free of the body, after spiritual liberation has been achieved.

Chapter III

Teaching of the Knowledge of Self

[*Comment*: Relationships of pain, pleasure and so forth, their cause and the order of removal; and by resorting to what, the removal is achieved, all that is expounded here.[1]]

The Lord said:

1. Hear further, O mighty-armed one, my highest words, which, out of a desire to benefit you, I shall speak to you, who are loving towards me.

   [*Comment*: In the last verse (Chapter II, verse 66) it was stated that those who are liberated from dichotomies such as the awareness of pleasure and pain, go to that state. What is the cause of (the spirit) joining these dichotomies, and what are the means of liberation? The Lord, wishing to instruct Arjuna in this, said: "Hear further", etc.

   "Loving" means desirous of listening with a happy mind and becoming satisfied by grasping the meaning of everything taught.]

2. Contacts with subtle elements, O son of Kuntī, only give heat and cold, pain and pleasure. They come and go, and are transient; therefore learn to withstand them.

   [*Comment*: To avoid a wrong impression of non-differentiation, i.e. the objects themselves are pain and pleasure, the commentator explains the etymology of the word *mātrā*: "those through which the object-experiences

---

[1] With this opening verse the commentator introduces and summarizes the argument of the chapter.

are measured" (*mīyante*). The Lord, accordingly, says that the *mātrā*s (the subtle elements) are the senses and the objects are measured by or through them. The contacts of the senses with the objects are the cause of pain and pleasure arising out of experiences such as cold and heat. *Sparśa*s (translated above as "contacts") are sounds and so forth, because they are contacted. Heat and cold are only referred to as analogies because the cool causes comfort in summer and heat causes pain, but later, in the cold season, it is the reverse. So the objects themselves are not experienced as pain and pleasure. Having shown the causes of pleasure and pain, he explains the means of learning to remove them, namely, learn to withstand them. Withstanding here may also indicate *vairāgya* (dispassion): be indifferent to the pleasant and bear the unpleasant neutrally.]

3. Those cannot happen to the one self and therefore where is pain or pleasure? How can any completion (by addition) or reduction take place, in that it is without a beginning and an end, and without any parts?

[*Comment*: The thoughts by which dispassion and forbearance are accomplished are explained. Those, i.e. the *mātrā*s, and contacts or pain and pleasure, and any other (relevant) factors, are not something other than one's own self, the one self whose nature is non-dual, perfect bliss. (It is by this thought that one attains dispassion and forbearance.) As to the possibility that one may assume pleasure by egoistic identity (*abhimāna*), out of confusion such as "I am made complete by a dear one, wealth, son and other advancements", and similarly that pain may arise with the thought that "I am reduced because of the unpleasant thing we call separation from those beloved things", such pain and pleasure also turn away when it is seen that the completion or reduction cannot take place in the One who is without any parts, to which, therefore, nothing can be added and from which nothing can be cut.]

4. In whom the contacts and the senses become settled (into stillness) and for whom the individual *jīva*-hood (is realized) only as falsehood of the senses and the contacts, such a wise man, alike in pleasure and pain, is ready for immortality.

   [*Comment*: For that wise man for whom the convictions of reality (or trueness) of "contacts", that is objects of senses, and of *mātrā*s, that is the senses, has ceased, for that wise man the (individual) *jīva*-hood consists only of (that) error concerning *mātrā*s and contacts. Such a wise man, seeing the true reality (*tattva*), becoming even in pain and pleasure, is then fit to (reach) immortality.]

5. Since the Self is all, these various beautiful divisions are as it were stopped, their form (in fact) non-existent, and how can a non-existing form not be bearable?

   [*Comment*: The question arises as to how it is possible that unpleasant pains and so forth may give up their nature of being averse to our feelings, so that they may become more bearable, and the answer is: since that one self, in whom the one enjoyment of unexcelled bliss is all, that self alone is all; then all these beautiful-appearing differentiations of pleasures and so forth merely appear as the divisions of beloved, wealth, son and so forth but do not produce sensations that are in discord to oneself (*pratikūla-vedanīyatā*). When this is known, they are, as it were, just stopped; therefore there is nothing that would be unbearable; they become unreal.]

6. Pains and pleasures entirely do not exist, even in the slightest, since the self, which is the essence, is all, how can there be existence of anything which is non-self?

7. There is no being of the non-existent, no non-being of the

existent; pleasures and pains and so forth do not exist; only the Supreme Self is the dweller in all.

[*Comment*: In this verse, the approach of the Vaiśeṣika and Nyāya schools is refuted, i.e. even though (originally) non-existent, etc. (a thing) may arise in the self, for a production is defined as something non-existent, which, because of inherence in it, may come into being at a certain given moment. (The view held here is) that non-existent pleasure and pain, etc. cannot have any existence at all. The existent cannot have non-existent existence, because a thing cannot exist in opposition to its own nature and also because passages such as *vācārambhana*[2] definitely state the unreality of all modification. The question arises, are we then not advocating the theory of *śūnya* (void) (as Buddhists do) since, there being no reality in all the modifications, there could not be any apprehension of things such as clay, because these things are perceivable only in the form of some modification? The answer is no (the *śūnya* view of the Buddhists is not being advocated). The objection regarding voidness is answered thus: the modified forms are unreal when the intelligence (*buddhi*) relating to them as real is (purified and) no longer has any objects of thought; that is not the same as void, otherwise it would follow (in the verses that) a pot is non-existent, a cloth is non-existent. What in fact follows, is that reality is existent (*sat sat*[3]), so (transcendentally speaking) only that reality remains; but the conscious attribution (*abhimāna*) to the modified forms that (this is real) persists only because of being permeated by the reality of the (higher) substratum and it is not their own. It is thus that pain, pleasure and so forth do not exist.]

---

2 *Chāndogya Upaniṣad* 6.1.

3 *Sat sat*, from the verb root *as*, "to be". *Sat* is the continuous participle meaning "existent". The word is also used to mean truth and reality.

8. Abandon opinions (as to) the reality and unreality of these, the world and the self; abandon also (what is in their) middle as "nothing", then fix[4] your mind on the remainder.

   [*Comment*: Abandon the thought of reality about the world and of the unreality of the self, which has unexcelled bliss; abandon also as insignificant what is between them as the means of joining them together, the mind and the darkness (*tamas*); then set your mind on what remains, the consciousness-self (*cid-ātman*). Fastened to that state, be well established in it.]

9. The self does not rejoice with pleasures, Arjuna, nor is it depressed by pains, though this conscious self (*cetana-ātmā*) remains within the body as a perceiver of the objects of perception.[5]

   [*Comment*: Perceives as witness, i.e. "remains seer of the seen". Those objects of perception cannot become (part of) the natures of the consciousness as witness.[6]]

10. The mind (*citta*), being unconscious (*jaḍa*), becomes subject to pain and so on, when it assumes identity with the body; when that is cut or diminished, nothing of the self diminishes.

11. If the unconscious (things) such as the body assume the position of being the experiencer of pain and such feeling,

---

[4] *Baddha-padaḥ*, established on one pedestal, one definite state of consciousness.

[5] *Dṛśya* and *dṛś*, the objects of perception, includes the physical body, mind and all the other material faculties, because *dṛś*, the seer, as pure self, is different from these, observing their functions and remaining a witness.

[6] *Dṛśya* and *dṛś*. These terms are fully explained in the *Yoga-Sūtras*. See our commentary of the same available from ahymsinpublishers@gmail.com

know that to be only a misapprehension through illusion (*māyā*), arising on account of ignorance.[7]

12. Nothing at all like body, nor such things as suffering, exist as separate from the self; then what is experienced, (and) by whom?

13. All this misapprehension vanishes through this, that which I am telling you here. Suffering is a misapprehension arising from ignorance, O Bharata, (and it vanishes) with perfect knowledge.

    [*Comment*: This thing called pain is a confusion arising out of the non-awakening (*a-bodha*). Therefore, it can be countered by correct and full awakening alone. Here I give an example (in next verse).]

14. Just as the fear of snake in a rope, born of ignorance (*a-bodha*), vanishes with awakening (to right knowledge) (*bodha*) (that it is no snake but a rope); so the suffering and so forth of body, born of ignorance, vanish with full enlightenment[8] (*samyag-bodha*).

15. Expansive in all directions, entire, unborn, the *Brahman* neither perishes nor is born; know this to be the highest truth; this is that supreme enlightenment (*bodha*).

16. In the *Brahman*-ocean the state of a wave just slightly comes into being and then dissolves; today you flash in the *Brahman*-whirl,[9] so you are the very *Brahman*.

    [*Comment*: Today: whenever the enlightenment comes, at that time.]

17. Whatever times, activities and orders are the soldiers of (the misconceptions of) "thou" and "I"; they are like vibrations

---

7 *A-bodha*, not being awake or enlightened.

8 *Samyag-bodha* (Sanskrit), reminiscent of Buddhist Pāli term *sammāsambodhi*.

9 Reminiscent of Vivartavāda of Vedānta.

in *Brahman*. There are no misapprehensions of reality and unreality about them.

[*Comment*: "Misapprehensions of reality and unreality", that is, there are no alternative possibilities (*vikalpa*) of their existence or non-existence.]

18. Give up (your) pride, frenzy, grief, fear, effort, comfort and discomfort; all this is dual, unreal by nature. Be one, with reality as your nature.

[*Comment*: The misapprehensions of "existent" and "non-existent": the alternatives of being and non-being.]

19. When the regiments of men perish as a nature of experience, it is (part of) *Brahman*'s expansiveness.[10] *Brahman* is pure. Perform your action as of *Brahman*.

[*Comment*: Even in the destruction of the regiments, to be undertaken by you, it is still the expanse of *Brahman*; so in your very experience as pure *Brahman*, perform the act (which is part) of *Brahman*.]

20. Having sensation of no pleasure and pain, gain or loss, victory or defeat,

21. Being alike in gain and loss, being indeed as nothing, just vibrating, like a pocket of air, undertake the duty that is at hand.

[*Comment*: Knowing the true essence you will be "nothing" — no form of body and so forth. Like a pocket of air separated in (a closed space such as) a cave (but in reality not separate from the air of the rest of the world).]

22. Whatever you do, whatever you eat, whatever you pour as a fire-offering, whatever you give, whatever you will do, be stabilized (in knowing), O son of Kuntī, all that is Self.

---

[10] Based on the normal etymology of *Brahman* as from verb root *bṛḥ*, to be large and vast, to be expansive. English word "big" is cognate to same.

[*Comment*: About all acts, "(this is) *Brahman* alone" — this determination being stable is the (meaning of) "surrender to me".]

23. Into whatever one becomes absorbed within, that without doubt he attains. To attain *Brahman*-truth, become absorbed in *Brahman*-truth.

[*Comment*: "Into whatever absorbed", i.e. whatever form one gives to one's mind (in meditation and otherwise).]

24. Becoming *Brahman*, in whom there is no expectation of fruit, contemplating it as *Brahman*, the action alone is performed as it comes by him who knows *Brahman*.

[*Comment*: The cessation of all desires, and that as the fruit, the final purpose, of being a person (*puruṣārtha*), the highest act. The action is performed (*vṛthā*, in vain, without seeking result) contemplating that the activity itself is *Brahman*.]

25. He who sees inaction in action and action in inaction, he is intelligent among men, and he is said to be the performer of complete action.

[*Comment*: The person who, in the manner prescribed in verse sees in his actions the *Brahman* who is without action, and who sees in the *Brahman* who is without action the action consisting of infallible and firm position, is the man endowed with intellect and discrimination. It is he alone who performs an action that is complete both in itself and in its results. Therefore he is called by the wise a doer of complete actions. This is the idea.]

26. Do not be a cause for the fruits of actions, (yet) do not be drawn towards inaction. Perform actions abiding in yoga, after abandoning attachment, O Dhanañjaya.

[*Comment*: Do not be a person whose motivations are the fruits of actions such as gains (derived from them). Do not let yourself be drawn to inaction, i.e. not undertaking what needs to be done on the spot. Abiding in yoga: maintaining an even view both towards success and failure, as stated above.]

27. Not resorting to attachment of actions, nor resorting to a stupor; nor even resorting to inaction, remain even and balanced (*sama*) and stable, just as you may be.

[*Comment*: Stupor: negligence in maintaining the view/ vision of reality.]

28. Abandoning attachment to the fruits of action, ever satiated, without any dependence, he who thus involves (himself) in action, does nothing at all.

29. Attachment is called the state of being a doer, which can accrue even to one who does nothing when the mind is dwelling in idiocy; one should therefore give up idiocy.

[*Comment*: Idiocy, as explained in the commentary to verse 27. In the presence of such idiocy, there will definitely be attachment, starting a chain of undesirable (developments).]

30. When a great-souled being (*mahātman*) is freed of attachment by resorting to the supreme knower of truth, then the state of doership does not accrue to him at all, even if he is absorbed in all (kinds of) activity.

[*Comment*: He says this is because otherwise the objection may arise that if one is not negligent in the realization of truth, is unattached, then he would naturally become inactive.]

31. From not being a doer, (proceeds) not being an experience. From not being an experiencer (proceeds) evenness, oneness. Through the even oneness, infinity; from that expands (into) the *Brahman*-state.[11]

---

[11] Attainment of union with *Brahman*.

[*Comment*: Thus through the succession of levels (attained, finally) the bodiless Absoluteness is perfected.]

32. Giving up the dross of multiplicity, having reached the Oneness of Supreme Self, even doing right or wrong action, you (will) not be a doer, O Arjuna.

    [*Comment*: Committing wrong prohibited acts, out of negligence.]

33. All of whose undertakings are free of passion and ideation, all his actions (karam) burnt in the fire of knowledge, him the wise call learned.

34. Even, of moonlike mien,[12] stable, always himself,[13] at peace, disinterested in all ends, he who remains thus is completely unagitated, even when agitated.

    [*Comment*: "Agitated" (means) involved in action; "unagitated" (means) actionless.

35. Free of dichotomies, ever remaining in harmony,[14] no gaining (yoga) or guarding (*kṣema*), endowed with self, accepting and following whatever comes your way, be you an ornament to the surface of the earth.

    [*Comment*: *Yoga*: attaining what is so far unattained. *Kṣema*: watching over what has been attained. Free of concern for both.]

36. He who, controlling the active senses, continues to contemplate with the mind the objects of the senses, is called a man of false character.

---

[12] *Saumya*, moon-like, water-like. A common compliment even in the modern languages of India. One whose presence imparts a moon-like feeling to others.

[13] *Svastha*, common word for one in good health, healthy. Literally, etymologically "self-abiding".

[14] *Nitya-sattva-stha*. Ever staying in *sattva*, the pure and harmonious state of mind. Or, remaining in eternal *sattva*.

[*Comment*: When a person has given up all (outward) activities, but the mind is not yet free of attachment, his renunciation is that of a hypocrite.]

37. The one, however, who, first controlling the senses with the mind, begins the yoga of action with the active senses (thus controlled with the mind), unattached, he is distinguished.

[*Comment*: A person of self-control over the mind and the senses, even performing actions as prescribed by the scripture, has the fruits of renunciation, because he had abandoned attachment to fruits. With this idea (Kr̥ṣṇa) praises him.]

38. As the waters enter the ocean, ever-filling, yet never changing its basin or bounds,[15] likewise, he whom all desires enter (like waters into depthless ocean) attains peace, not one who desires desires.

[*Comment*: Just as waters enter and vanish in the sea that is ever filled, becoming one with its being, so all desires enter that renunciate who has his establishment in the firm *Brahman*. (These desires enter him), their realm negated by (his) intellection of (their) falsity. Thus they vanish in him, become one with the self alone. Only such a person attains liberation, which is marked with tranquillity, not the person who is inclined towards desiring objects.]

In the Great Rāmāyaṇa of Vasiṣṭha, composed by Vālmīki as narrated by a messenger of *devas*, the Path to Liberation, Nirvāṇa Section in the Narrative of Arjuna end of the fifty-fourth (54th) chapter.

---

15 *Pratiṣṭhā* may mean both "basin" and "bank".

Chapter IV

The Determination of the Nature of Jīva

[*Comment*: Not destroyed even at the destruction of the body, (Self is) the same in the fool and the philosopher; the fool goes through births and so forth, but not so he who knows; this is explained here.]

The Lord said:

1. One should neither relinquish enjoyment[1] nor cultivate enjoyment; one should remain even and the same, accepting whatever comes (his way).

   [*Comment*: The enjoyments (*bhoga*s) are (so called because) they are experienced as the means of maintaining the body; food and drink, for example. One should not give these up, i.e. one should take the food and so forth that is beneficial in the right measure and pure (*hita, mita, medhya*). One should not give thought to those enjoyments (so that) refining them (becomes) an addiction. One should remain completely even, whether he gains or does not gain those (enjoyments).]

2. Do not develop[2] a consideration of self-ness in the body, whose nature is to become.[3] Develop a consideration of

---

[1] *Bhoga*, experience as a means or as a result of action.

[2] *Bhāvaya*, develop the *bhāvanā* by contemplating.

[3] *Bhavātman*, whose self is *bhava* (the worldly being) and going through the six modifications of being which is meant by "becoming", going through the processes of modifications.

self-ness only in the true self, whose nature it is not to become.

[*Comment*: "Whose nature it is to become", i.e., whose nature undergoes the modifications (*vikriyā*, changes or products) such as birth.]

3. In the loss[4] of the body, O mighty-armed one, nothing at all is lost. Only the loss of self may be (called) a loss, but (as a matter of fact) the self is never lost.[5]

4. The self, not to be identified with mind (*citta*), is not shattered[6] (when) it has relinquished all grasping; even when undertaking action he does nothing at all.

[*Comment*: Having stated that view, now supporting the authority of such textual passages (Śruti) as "Indestructible, he is not shattered"(*Bṛhadāraṇyaka Upaniṣad* 6.5.15) he says (in the verse) that only the grasping through false identity (*abhimāna*) can occasion (*prasaṅga*) of the (erroneous attribution of) destructibility and so forth to the self.

The self not identified with the mind (*acittātman*), i.e. (the self) is seen through discrimination as separate from the mind (*citta*), which is the instrument of grasping of the body, etc.

[*Comment*: Action: that is (forthcoming) battle, etc.]

5. (It is) attachment they call being a doer, and that can belong even to one who does nothing when the mind is dwelling in foolishness. Therefore, one should be rid of foolishness.[7]

---

4 *Naś*, perish. The verb root *naś* is cognate with English "loss".

5 Emphasizes that self and mind are not identical.

6 Verb root *śṝ*, to be shattered or scattered, to get spilled. The body is called *śarīra* because its components decompose and scatter whereas the self is free of such "being scattered".

7 This verse is identical to verse 29 of Chapter 3.

[*Comment*: "Dwelling in foolishness", i.e. fallen into ignorance.]

6. When a great soul (*mahātmā*) resorts to the Supreme Knower of that-ness, and has no attachment, then, even if he is absorbed in all actions, no (assumption of) being a doer arises for him anywhere.[8]

7. (The wise) knows the self to be indestructible, with no beginning, no end, no decay. "The self perishes" — let not such a pain-giving wrong thought come to you.

   [*Comment*: The means of freeing oneself from the stupor (advised in verse 5) are explained here (in verses 6 and 7).]

8. The highest ones, who have known the self, do not see this way. They do not see their self (confused) with non-self. Contemplating *ātman* the self, they see the self in the self.

   [*Comment*: They do not see "the self perishes". Why? Because they meditate on the self in the self. They do not see the non-self, such as the body, as the self.]

Arjuna said:

9. O Lord of the three worlds, who gives honour even to the ignorant, if that is so, then when the body is ready to perish, nothing desirable is destroyed.

   [*Comment*: Arjuna expressed doubt: fools may see the body and so forth as self, still, when their (bodies, etc.) perish, the self does not perish, and death and so forth cannot be undesirable.]

The Lord said:

10. Thus it is, O mighty-armed one, that nothing perishes anywhere. The self indeed is the very self of non-destruction; what of it, where, ever perishes?

---

[8] This verse is identical to verse 30 of Chapter 3.

[*Comment*: The Lord answers with *iṣṭāpatti*.[9]]

11. This is lost, this is found; all this, I see nothing else except but misapprehension through delusion, such as "the son of a barren woman".

[*Comment*: How then is the perishing of the body and the birth of a son be undesirable or desirable? Well, one has the delusion of a son's birth or death even in a dream.]

12. There is no being of the non-existent, no non-being of the existent; those who see the essence see the end of both of these.

[*Comment*: As has already been said above, since real cannot be non-existent, the personality and so forth do not have a reality. The real is only real, the unreal is only unreal. They cannot exchange their very nature. This conclusion is drawn by those who have seen the true essence, but not by those who are deluded.]

13. However, know that to be indestructible by which all this is pervaded; no-one can bring about the destruction of this immutable one.

14. These bodies of that eternal body-owner, the indestructible and immeasurable one, are taught as having an end; therefore fight, O Bhārata.[10]

[*Comment*: (On verses 13 and 14): Thus what is real is indestructible; what is destructible is only unreal. In this sense, there is no great calamity when the bodies, etc. of the kinsmen are lost in the battle, since they are in this sense unreal.]

15. The one alone, the self, exists; there is no two-ness; then how can non-existent (unreal) have a being? That self

---

9 *Iṣṭāpatti*, a device in logic, "A statement by a debater, which is favourable to his opponent also" (Apte's *Sanskrit–English Dictionary*).

10 Verses 12-14 are the same as *Bhagavad-Gītā* 2.16-18.

is indestructible, without an end, and there can be no destruction of the existent (real).

[*Comment*: Since there is no "two", there can be no-one who is a destroyer of the first; therefore the self cannot be destroyed (by any other).]

16. After abandoning the two-ness and the one-ness, the remainder is the tranquil, the middle between the existent (real) and the non-existent (unreal): that here is the supreme state.

[*Comment*: One-ness is the source-cause, signified by the word *sat* (existent, real); two-ness is the effect-product *asat* (non-existent, unreal) the untrue. Between those two is the Real alone, the substratum.]

Arjuna said:

17. Then what causes men to take the position, "I am dying"? And, how do those heaven and hell happen to be for the people, O Lord?

[*Comment*: Arjuna asks: what is the reason for the confusion of delimited sorrow and so forth, and death and so on about the undelimited self? For what reason has it arisen? *sthiti*, i.e. *niyati* (destiny).[11] In that *sthiti* what creates the hell that is suffering and heaven that is pleasure?

The Lord said:

18. Earth, water, fire, air, space, mind and intelligence; having just these (modifications of) subtle elements (*tan-mātras*) as his net, the individual spirit (*jīva*) dwells in the body.

[*Comment*: To explain the text (Śruti) "arising from these elements he perishes along with them" [*etebhyo bhūtebhyaḥ samutthāya tāny evānu vi naśyati* . . .], the Lord states that the Supreme becomes a *jīva*, which simply means taking on

11 Literally, a stand, situation or position.

the identity of individual and collective gross and subtle bodies made up of mind, intelligence and so forth, which are the measures of the five subtle elements, and that alone is the reason for the fate that is the delusion of birth, death, pleasure, pain, and so forth.]

19. He is pulled by the propensity (*vāsanā*) like the young of cattle by a rope; he dwells inside the body like a bird in a cage.

[*Comment*: He explains the reason for the self taking on the variegated bodies and acting according to the body of each (species he occupies).]

20. When the body comes to infirmity because of the force of time and place, then under the power of the *vāsanās* he goes away, like juices squeezed from the leaf of a fig-tree (*Ficus religiosa*).

[*Comment*: The *vāsanā* alone is the means of transmigration from a previous body to the following one.]

21. (The consciousness of) ear, eye, touch, taste and smell; taking these along he goes as a breeze taking the scent from their sources.

[*Comment*: *Āśaya*[12] (source), the previous body, such as a flower.]

22. The body is nothing but his being joined with *vāsanās*; it is born of no other arrangement. It wanes and vanishes[13] upon the renunciation of *vāsanās*; when it vanishes, that state (transcendental) comes to be.

---

12 *Āśaya* is anything in which some attribute may remain dormant for a time, for example, *āmāśaya* is the place of undigested food, the stomach; *karmāśaya* is the place of karam in the subtle body before it comes to its maturity and begins to bear fruit.

13 Verb root *kṣi*, to dissipate slowly and then vanish completely.

[*Comment*: The gross body, too, consists only of *vāsanā* only. Because of its continuity for a long period there is misapprehension of its concreteness. When *liṅga* (the subtle body) vanishes, the highest state takes over naturally, of its own accord.]

23. This *jīva* Being endowed with the *vāsanā*s and borne by the Supreme, wanders in the species, bearing the burden of delusion like a magical (unreal) man.[14]

[*Comment*: The Supreme himself, who has become the individual, supports (this personality) with food, drink, and so on: the *liṅga* (subtle body), endowed with propensities, is doubly borne by the transcendental self, who has entered it himself, taking forms both ways, that is, delimitation (*avaccheda*) and becoming a reflexion (*pratibimba*), thus supported doubly. Both the personality and the individual self are manifestation of that one magical man, (not real), yet moving about in the sky by some magic.

24. The individual soul (*jīva*), under the power of *vāsanā*s, takes from the body all the natures of the senses and migrates like a breeze (taking) fragrance from a flower.

[*Comment*: This is further explanation of verse twenty-one. "Natures" means the powers (*śakti*) to apprehend sound and so forth.]

25. When the *jīva* has migrated, O son of Kuntī, all waxing of the organs ceases all vibration, like a tree whose expansive span of limbs becomes still when the wind calms down.

26. It becomes (gradually) invisible because of (its natural) faults, such as breaking and bursting deterioration. The body, from which thereby the life is gone, is then called "dead"; motionless.

---

[14] The way a man is seen performing tricks up in space in a magic show. This is from the ancient *indrajāla* tradition of magic.

[*Comment*: And that is what people call death.]

27. Wherever in space that *jīva*, from having *prāṇa* as its image (or form), comes to be, he sees that very form as an extension (of his *vāsanās*), because of the habit of his *vāsanās*.

    [*Comment*: In the space that is in the consciousness-space (*cid-ākāśa*) or in physical space, wherever his *vāsanās* become aroused, in the way of his being an experiencer as to the forms of things being experienced, such as body, place, time, objects of experience and so forth, he sees that very form (and assumes it).

28. Upon its destruction, this very body is seen by the *jīva* as if non-existent. You, too, see it as if nothing, like a man asleep.[15]

    [*Comment*: See the non-existence and unreality as upon the destruction of the body, or as a person asleep does not see this body as real.]

29. Just as he sees those forms, so also he sees their destructions because of the repeated disposition (*bhāvanā*)[16] — coming from the disposition established in the beginning of creation, indeed.

    [*Comment*: Just as these (physical) counterparts are produced by *vāsanā*, so too their destructions have been brought about from the beginning of the (cycles of) creation. So he says, "Just as he. . . ." At the beginning of creation, Brahmā brought about the forms of cow, horses and so forth from the propensities arising from the experience of previous cycles of creation. All this is done through the repeated disposition in his imagination and not like a potter taking up clay and stick and so on. The force of "indeed" here is

---

15 Compare *Yoga-Sūtras* of Patañjali 1.38. One may reach *samādhi* by concentrating on the state of sleep or dream.

16 See Chapter 2, verse 22 *et seq*.

that it is well known in the inspired texts (Śruti), texts of narrative (Purāṇas), etc.]

30. Immediately upon production or perception (*udbhava*), whatever is seen before one, in whatever way, remains the same, and, in his awareness of that, the same change inheres until the fall (dissolution) in the awareness (*saṁvid*) of a relationship of *sine qua non* (*avinābhāvi-saṁvid*).]

[*Comment*: *Objection*: At the time of creation, the universe consisting of *vāsanā*s may be false, but in its continuity it must be regarded as real, as we see (all objects in it) efficacious as to their purpose and because its reality is experienced in common by all people.

Answer: Whatever form, such as the body or a pot[17] thought of as seen in whatever way in the first moment, whether false or real, it does not change its nature to the last. It continues in the same form as it was produced at first, because its substratum is its *sine qua non* (*avinā-bhāvitā*), the consciousness in which the object experienced inheres, without which its reality is not experienced.]

31. A previous route of the *vāsanā* is overcome by personal effort (*puruṣārtha*) as yesterday's situation is quickly (changed) by today's effort.

[*Comment*: Well, let the personalities and so forth consist of *vāsanā*s; so what? The stanza answers, a total eradication of the form of personality, etc., which was imagined from the evil *vāsanā*, occurs through the force of becoming one with *Brahman*, which comes about by the practice of good *vāsanā*. It is "overcome", i.e. prevented, through knowledge of the indivisible nature, through a person's effort (being) dedicated to listening, meditating, etc. (on

[17] Or, body as the clay pot. The analogy of the body and a pot of clay is very common in Vedānta texts.

the right teachings), just as yesterday's transgression of the principles of virtue (*adharma*) is conquered by today's effort in the observance of expiations and so forth, or a yesterday's thatched house is burned by today's endeavour at arson.]

32. Whatever personal effort is seen (at the first) moment by a man of strength, that (strong) part of the preceding and following actions (finally) clearly wins.

[*Comment*: *Objection*: Often the efforts of many people for knowledge are overcome by the strong prior *vāsanā*s of desire, anger, and so forth. Therefore, (today's effort is not always capable of overcoming yesterday's *vāsanā*s and) in the sequence of time, it is of no consequence. The stanza explains: through his *abhiniveśa*,[18] whichever one of the *puruṣārtha*s[19] — *dharma*, *artha*, *kāma* and *mokṣa* — one realizes one's direction to be, that special part of his preceding and following (determination and) effort brings forth victory. When the *abhiniveśa* towards liberation is weak, and towards worldly experiences is strong, then one suffers defeat.]

33. Even when the Vindhya mountain is exploding or the winds of dissolution are blowing, personal effort is

---

[18] *Abhiniveśa*, this word is used in the *Yoga-Sūtras* in the sense of inhibition against death; the desire to continue to be alive in the same body. Here, however, the word has been used in a different sense to denote the force of one's propensities, which gives one an unconscious direction, impels one, as if it were a compulsion. Please see discussion on the word both in vols. 1 and 2 of our commentary on the *Yoga-Sūtras of Patañjali*, available from ahymsinpublishers@gmail.com

[19] *Puruṣārtha*s, the four endeavours of man: *dharma*, religious, moral and philanthropic pursuit in the path of virtue; *artha*, worldly means in a social, political, economic, financial areas of life; *kāma*, desires and passions, also, when kept under control, as through marital life; and *mokṣa*, liberation.

enjoined by the scriptures and should not be given up by a man of wisdom.

[*Comment*: Therefore one should strengthen the *abhiniveśa* toward the effort prescribed by the scriptures.]

34. Because of the forces of the *vāsanā*s of hell, heaven, creation and so forth, the *jīva*, with his wisdom (influenced by) an old solid delusion, sees before him what has been practised for long.

[*Comment*: When one's inclination towards (such high effort) is weak, because of the force of a variety of previous *vāsanā*s, the chain of misfortunes, of pains and pleasures, is very difficult to ward off. "The wisdom influenced by old solid delusion" means the faculty of discrimination deluded by the original ignorance.[20]]

Arjuna said:

35. O Lord of the universe, do tell me what is the cause of the *jīva*'s stay of the world (which consists of) the confusions of hell, heaven, creation and so forth?

[*Comment*: Arjuna asks these questions so that he may clearly understand the same idea by way of refuting a doubt about another reason put forward in the words of Vyāsa and others, which say:

"This ignorant creature having no power over his own pain or pleasure may go to heaven or hell as impelled by God."[21]

---

20 *Anādi-vāsanā* or *anādi avidyā* (the eternal ignorance) is a doctrine peculiar to Vedānta philosophy. It is a function of *māyā*, which is *Brahman*'s potential to create an illusion of the manifold universe and beings, within its own pure being. See the commentary on verse 41.

21 *Mahābhārata*, Āraṇyakaparvan, 31.27.

"The stay", i.e. the *jīva* who is the cause of the stay of the world.]

The Lord said:

36. The *vāsanā* is like a dream; (only) elimination of *vāsanā* (leads to) the highest good. When it becomes mature (strong) because of long practice, it causes the misapprehension of *saṁsāra*.

[*Comment*: Do not try to find another reason. Because God, passion, action, and so forth also bring about pain and pleasure in accordance with *vāsanā* alone, this (*vāsanā*) only is the uncommon cause (*hetu*) of the worldly cycle (*saṁsāra*), (when) it grows strong through long habit. So, only its elimination should be pursued, with all possible effort, by one who has accepted the supreme end of man (*parama-puruṣārtha*). Making this clear, the Lord says, "like a dream"; i.e. because by one not following the injunctions of the scripture, the dream-like *vāsanā* alone becoming strong, produces (literally "gives forth") the error of the world. Therefore, total elimination of *vāsanā* from the root through the practice of philosophy (*tattva-jñāna*, knowledge of the true essence) leads to the *summum bonum*. This (is how the verse) fits together.]

Arjuna said:

O Lord God of gods, from what does the *vāsanā* arise, and how is it eliminated?

The Lord said:

37. The *vāsanā* arises from the stupor of ignorance (and) consists of the contemplation of self in non-self. It goes to (its) dissolution through the great enlightenment (*mahā-bodha*), (which is) the knowledge of the self.

[*Comment*: Ignorance alone is the root of *vāsanā* and by knowledge alone it can be eliminated from the root.]

38. You have contemplated the self, O son of Kuntī, and you have truly gained knowledge. "This", "he", "I", "these people by me" — give up such *vāsanā*s.

[*Comment*: Through contemplation you have reached acquaintance with the nature of the self. Now, by strengthening it, you only need to eliminate the *vāsanā* as to the body, and the kinsmen related to it, "I", "mine", and so on. That remains to be accomplished.]

Arjuna said:

39. At the dissolution of the *vāsanā*s, the *jīva* himself (would) be dissolved; whatever waxes from the existence of something by the loss of it is dissolved.

[*Comment*: Since the *liṅga* (the subtle body) consists of *vāsanā*s in which the *jīva* is experienced as a reflection, then on the loss of the *vāsanā*s the *jīva* also would be dissolved; so this "true knowledge" can only lead to a predicament.

40. When the *jīva* has come to dissolution and the place and time have changed, then who is it that becomes the medium of birth and death?

[*Comment*: Birth and death, not in the ordinary sense, but the birth (that is) the supreme goal of the person, which is the appearance of the highest bliss, and the death (that is) the final dissolution of the totality of predicaments, because one who knows the truth had eradicated his *vāsanā*s totally and can have no ordinary birth and death because that would be in discord with the context of the teaching of (this) text.]

The Lord said:

41. Having created the resolution (*saṅkalpa*) through his own will, that aspect of self which just becomes obscured, taking the form of *vāsanā*s, know that to be the *jīva*, O you of great intelligence.

[*Comment*: The Lord replies. The objection (raised by Arjuna) would be right if the *jīva* were in the worldly cycle merely as a reflection (*pratibimba*). Such a *jīva* would then be thought of as some other than the original (*bimba*, whose reflexion it is), divided into time, space, etc. and of birth and so on, which are dependent on the subtle elements (*bhūta-mātrā*). But that is not the case. *Brahman* alone, which is transcendentally pure, obscured (*pihitam*[22]) by its own untrue ignorance, not knowing its essence (*tattvam*), goes into worldly cycles (*saṁsarati*, transmigrates) within itself by imagining the differentiation of soul and the world (*jīva* and *jagat*). That very (*Brahman*), coming to know its true essence through the endeavour of listening to scriptures and so forth, shaking off the ignorance that was accompanying the *vāsanā*, (again) settles down into its own being (*svabhāva*) and that alone is its liberation. This is the view of the scripture (Śruti). There none of the objections raised by you applies.]

42. Not dependent, without ideation, the immutable nature of self, becoming free of *vāsanā*s through full enlightenment, know that to be liberation, O Bhārata.

43. Even alive (in this body)[23] O mighty-armed one, see this essence as it stands; freed from the reins of *vāsanā*s, he is called liberated.

[*Comment*: That state of eradication of all *vāsanā*s while remaining in the body is called *jīvan-mukti*. It can be

---

[22] *Pihitam*, closed, covered. Cf. *Īśa Upaniṣad*, verse 17: "The face of Truth is covered with a golden lid." So ignorance is an untruth on a cosmic scale, and the commentator, Ānanda-Bodhendra, used here the term *anṛta* to qualify *avidyā* (ignorance). *Anṛta* in the Vedas is the opposite of *ṛta*, meaning the truth of the cosmic laws, as against mere *satya* (relative truth).

[23] Kṛṣṇa means to say that Arjuna should aim at seeking liberation while in the current body.

experienced even by you right here; therefore you should have no doubt about the possibility of liberation.]

44. One who is not voided of *vāsanās*, even though performing all virtuous observances, even though knowing everything, is bound from all sides, like a bird kept in a cage.

[*Comment*: And that liberation cannot be attained by acts, nor by scholarship of things visible as external objects, but by knowledge of self alone. So he says, "One who is not . . ." etc.]

45. Only he whose *vāsanā* flashes within and (gradually thins down, becomes very fine), as a man with a bad eye seeing peacocks tails in the sky, he alone becomes liberated (*mukta*); here indeed *vāsanā* alone is bondage (which the liberated man) does not have, for its elimination is liberation.

[*Comment*: "One with bad eyes" or the self (whose eyes) are closed by his own *māyā* and who has not yet found the authority of the teachings of Vedānta. In the sky of the supreme self, the subtle *vāsanā*, the source of many confusions, flashes like a magic peacock's tail and becomes an extension in the form of *jīva* and the universe (*jīva-jagat*). The same *jīva* coming into the personality of an *adhikārin* (one who is a ready recipient of the teaching), the true knowledge arising in him, becomes liberated from the bondage of *vāsanā* from its very roots. "Here" means in this supreme self. (The first flash of very subtle *vāsanā* appears in the supreme self, and that is the first origin of ignorance and the very root of the *vāsanā* of the *jīva* and the universe.)]

In the Great Rāmāyaṇa of Vasiṣṭha, composed by Vālmīki as narrated by a messenger of *devas*, the Path to Liberation,
Nirvāṇa Section in the
Narrative of Arjuna
end of the fifty-fifth (55th) canto.

Chapter V

Description of Mind

[*Comment*: In this chapter is being taught to Arjuna: to become established in liberation while living (*jīvan-mukti*), essence and reality of the consciousness and existence, image of the world and the mind mural.]

The Lord said:

1. Thus becoming free of the *vāsanā*s as one liberated-in-life (*jīvan-mukta*), O Arjuna, reaching the coolness within, abandon the maculation (of the thought of) the pain of (your) kinsmen (in the battle).

   [*Comment*: "Pain of kinsmen", your pain concerning the death of kinsmen (in battle).]

2. Having no fear of old age and death, your inner personality (*āśaya*) clear like the sky, giving up all ideations concerning the desirable and the undesirable, be free of all attractions (*rāga*[1]), O sinless one.

3. This duty, whatever, however, it has come flowing along in the flux,[2] must be performed. Perform the actions that must be done; nothing at all is lost here.

   [*Comment*: "Flowing in the flux", i.e. as handed down as a tradition of the behaviour of those (noble) people who were well taught. Perform your duty, such as the battle,

1 "That which closely accompanies and follows an experience of pleasure is *rāga*." — *Yoga-Sūtras*, 2.7.

2 *Pravāha*, the natural flow of an order such as the universe and its laws, karam and its fruition.

as well as other sacraments and charities; you will not lose any of your enlightenment thereby.]

4. Whatever is one's own duty, that comes along in the flux, is performed. This is the nature of one liberated-in-life, and that is liberation in life.

   [*Comment*: One's own action; that is consisting of one's own *dharma*. Such is the nature of *jīvan-mukti*, not merely the abandoning of the movements of the body.]

5. "I give up this act", "I resort to this act", such determination is the condition of mind in stupor; a wise man's state is constant.

6. Performing acts as they come along in the flux, with their minds pacific, abiding in sleep, the *jīvan-mukta*s (continue to) flash like a man asleep.

   [*Comment*: They abide in sleep, i.e. like someone asleep they remain devoid of ideation with the self. They flash a pure self of self-luminous light, like the self of a man asleep, with only the self remaining.]

7. Whose senses by nature come to a steady state from the objects of sense, into the heart, like the limbs of a tortoise, from all directions (is *jīvan-mukta*).

   [*Comment*: A further similarity with sleep in the state of *jīvan-mukta* is explained in this stanza. Because they are opposed by knowledge, the senses automatically, without effort, turn away from the objects of the insignificant senses. "In the heart", i.e. in the supreme self dwelling in the heart. They come to a steady state together with mind. Just as the head, feet and so forth of a tortoise are drawn in very quickly, even at the slightest agitation outside, such is the nature of a *jīvan-mukta*. What happens is that not only a *jīvan-mukta*, but even one aspiring and travelling on the path, has a different reaction to the objects of the senses.

Where an ordinary man's mind is drawn toward them as he sees them, the natural response of an aspirant towards such a stimulus is to withdraw immediately into the inner self.]

8. In the universal spirit-mind, the painter of mind-image(s) creates a mural without a wall — the universe with three worlds, divided into three divisions of time.

[*Comment*: Then how do the *jīvan-mukta*s see the world and interact with it in ordinary practice? The stanza shows that they do so like the variegated non-wall mural brought about by imagination in the mind-kingdom. The entire universe from beginning to end of creation is in the form of a painting created by the mind, in the mind.[3] The artisan, defined as mind, creator of the painting, paints the mural called "the three worlds" without a wall — the whole universe commonly known among all people as being of endless variety. He paints it in the self that is the substratum of all in the universe (*viśva*).]

9. In the (empty) sky, made even of (empty) space, (painted) clear with pastels of *vṛtti*s, in the beginning (of creation), Oh, a strange painting was first spread out by mind, the painter!

[*Comment*: "In the sky" of ignorance; "consisting of space", that is, something that can have no magnitude, because it consists only of ignorance. The painting is spread out, made with pastels consisting of the *vṛtti*s of the inner sense (*antaḥkaraṇa*), in which (the phantom) reflects.

10. (A splendid painting was first made), and then the wall, which is space, was created; Oh, what confusion! Unique is this great magic, the excessive *māyā*, this beautiful (magic) of a wall made of straw.

---

3 *Mano-racita-citra*— the same phrase is translated both as "created by the mind" and "in the mind".

[*Comment*: Expresses wonder by demonstrating the contrariety (of the process of this painting) with the commonly known paintings. The collective mind, because its ideation is a true one[4] (*satya-saṅkalpa*), created the world-painting simultaneously with the arising of the ideation and then created the wall, which should be the base of some mural. And strange, a wall completely incapable of sustaining the mural, for it is made up of formless space, as incapable, devoid of any essence, as a wall made of straw.]

11. There is not the slightest difference between the two (objects of) apprehension (the wall and the mural), as these walls are experienced arising in the very painting in the mind.

[*Comment*: He shows another wonder: "not the slightest difference". In ordinary murals, there are walls separate from the painting. Here, however, the walls, such as space, are noticed arising in the painting in the mind. Thus both the support (wall) and the supported (the painting), are not in the least different from the mind itself.]

12. O lotus-eyed one, know those (walls) even more void than (empty) space as both the creation and dissolution of the world pass confusing in the mind within a moment.

[*Comment*: From "Oh confusion" (verse 10) "Oh" was explained (in verse 11) and now he explains the confusion. Those compositions of mental paintings are voider than space, i.e. absolutely unreal. There he uses the illustration of momentary trinity of worlds: *kṣaṇa* (moment) is (a time division); the sixth part of the hour of a water-clock.[5]

---

4 While the wishes arising in weak and untruthful minds are seldom fulfilled, a strong mind creates everything by ideation (*saṅkalpa*).

5 A *ghaṭikā* was the ancient device for measuring time. A curved plate with a carefully measured hole in the bottom floated on water. The time it took to sink down was a *ghaṭikā*. Two-and-a-half *ghaṭikā*s make the modern hour. Here the commentator defines *kṣaṇa*, moment as →

13. The Self alone is this entire universe, as well as the space within and without.

Because this is a mind-kingdom of long duration, therefore indeed (the appearance of) reality.

[*Comment*: (Translated differently) the self here is the mind, and creation is the world and the space, like a dream, is void and unreal. Why then do people have an appearance of reality? Because this (dream) is of long duration. The force of "indeed" here is to emphasize that "this is not true reality".

14. Can there be any reality when nothing is seen? There is never any reality in a delirium.

As one looks at a reality with the help of sunshine, gradually with the (same) sunshine (the same) reality disappears.

[*Comment*: How can there be any reality before the real essence is realized, since there is no reality in all three times in any objects which are imagined through misapprehension? *Krameṇa* (gradually) means in the order of times and seasons and states such as childhood, or in the order of six modifications of being (*bhāva-vikāra*). The reality that is commonly seen as empirical in the practical world, or as the efficacy of objects, all disappears in the light that is the realization of the true essence; just as a patch of mist is seen in the light of the sun and is later dried up by the same sunshine.]

15. A patch of mist in the winter diminishes right in front of one's eyes.

→ one-sixth part of a *ghaṭikā*. However, in deeper philosophy, a *kṣaṇa* is the time it takes the finest atomic particle to traverse its own length (see Vyāsa's commentary on *YS* 3.52, and Vācaspati on same). That "moment" seems more appropriate in the context here.

In the painting of the mind-painter exist the picture-puppets.

[*Comment*: So, only through the false notion of the mind-painting all the affliction of the slaying of the kinsmen and so forth is possible.]

16. There being no walls (for this mural), the three worlds and so forth have no forms outside (the mind); neither they nor you exist (as separate individual reality). What is made to cease? By whom?

[*Comment*: "Made to cease", killed.]

17. Give up the delusion of the slain and the slayer, and be pure in space. Because space can have no operations and the operation itself is (void as) space.

[*Comment*: "In the space", *Brahman*-space. The consciousness space (*cid-ākāśa*) cannot have operations such as slaying and the apparent operation is one with the space that is *Brahman*. The illusory (*prātibhāsikī*)[6] involvement itself is of the form of space, i.e. *Brahman*-space.]

18. Therefore (this) space is clear of time, actions, and art on the walls and so forth; it is the self of the entire (universe and its forms) like a painting that has taken form remaining in the mind.

[*Comment*: This space, *Brahman*, as the picture of a mind-kingdom, has all the details in the mind, yet it is like space. So the universe, though visible, is even more void than space.]

---

[6] In Vedānta, one speaks of three levels of reality: (1) *pāramārthikī*, transcendental reality in which *Brahman* is the only reality, in which snake and rope are both in *Brahman*, (2) *vyāvahārikī*, empirical existence of the world through the force of *māyā* in which snake is a snake and rope is a rope, and (3) *prātibhāsikī*, illusory existence in which for a moment a rope is mistaken for a snake in the dark. In this verse, even the *vyāvahārikī* is seen as *prātibhāsikī*.

19. Similarly, know this world to be even more void than space,

A picture produced on the wall of the mind by the consciousness (*cit*) as painter.

[*Comment*: The unknown consciousness now is the painter and the mind its wall. Even by this analogy only voidness of the universe can be concluded.]

20. Because of its being totally void no (piece) of space can be broken off.

Therefore the creation and destruction of the world appear in the mind.

[*Comment*: Here, too the same analogy applies, that of momentary universe in the kingdom of the mind.]

21. So within this moment, know that these (the thought of slayer and the slain) on this earth (also) are void.

Oh, today all this imagination in the mind-kingdom, which consists of a variety of experiences, has vanished.

[*Comment*: The imagination of there being a slayer or slain that was produced by momentary delusion in your mind-kingdom has today vanished through my teaching.]

22. This imagination has been created through the delusions arising from a moment's contemplation, since the mind is capable of creating a totally non-existent mind-kingdom.

[*Comment*: The question arises: how could a moment's delusion have created the mind-kingdom defined as the world, stretching through the beginningless and endless aeons (*kalpa*)? He says that since the mind is capable of producing non-existent birth, it is also capable of turning a moment into aeons.]

23. The mind has similarly the power to turn a moment into an aeon (*kalpa*[7]);

[7] One cycle of creation and dissolution.

It turns a moment into an aeon and makes the little into much.

[*Comment*: That it (the mind) makes a moment into an aeon and gives birth to the non-existent (world), this wonder is merely a minor one. Even greater wonder is that it turns the non-existent world (as it were) into an existent one. By such power of the mind this error of the (existence of the) world has risen.]

24. It makes the non-existent very quickly existent, so this confusion has arisen;

Within a moment the mind-kingdom shines forth from (mind's) own nature.

25. So, strange in itself, is this net of the universe; this is definite.

It has risen like the blink of an eye from its adherence to *nirvāṇa*, even in its very creation.

Comment: Though the self is "(in) *nirvāṇa*", i.e. ever free (*nitya-mukta*), and the universe, momentary as the wink of an eye, has arisen in it merely as a sudden (mental) reflection, confused people have imagined a solid reality that cannot easily be terminated. That is not correct; so he says "mere shining forth". Even though the world is insignificant and lasting only a moment, a mere eye-wink, by the ignorant who do not know (reality) has been imagined an admantine concreteness, difficult to erase.]

26. Though it is a mere shining forth,[8] adamantine[9] concreteness has been attributed to it,

It is only an error in the light[10] of one who does not know the real form.

---

8 *Pratibhā* whereby an idea or image flashes in the mind. The same words may be used for flashes on a screen.

9 *Vajrasāratā*, the quality of the heart of diamond or steel.

10 *Pratibhāsa*, as *pratibhā*.

[*Comment*: When the self does not know the real essence, this world, which is the reverse of its true light, appears; how can such adamantine concreteness be imagined in such an "operativeness" (*pravṛtti*), i.e. superimposition (*adhyāropa*) or in its "cessation" (*nivṛtti*), i.e. refutation (of the superimposition)? None whatsoever.]

27. How can such adamantine reality be assumed about the turning on or turning off of the operations?

When did the universe-picture of mind the painter ever remain in the consciousness (*cit*)?

[*Comment*: An effort is required in eradication of something that holds a steady existence. (One may need to refute that but) this (picture in the mind) never remains of steady existence anywhere.]

28. Without a wall, without a provision of colours, here is like an expanse before us.

Oh, strange, the mural without a wall stands out very clear. This is a wonder.

[*Comment*: Unreal, because it has no material[11] cause, and unreal in itself; yet it flashes before us. Colours, such as blue and yellow, colour materials used in creating a painting.]

29. Oh, how entertaining and of beautiful colours is this world, so clear, attractive to the sight, with many lines drawn in the ink of darkness (*tamas*), colourful with the rays of many splendours.

[*Comment*: "Entertaining" (*rañjanam*), that which makes us very well attached. (Sight) represents (all the) senses, mind and so forth.]

30. With many limbs of the cycles (of creation, *kalpas*) and their parts (*yugas*, aeons), painted with colours of many

---

11 Material, i.e. the implements required for painting, such as colours.

attractions (*rāgas*), rich with the luxury of many views, interesting for its many experiences.

31. With the fierce splendour of many celestial bodies, with many forms in east and west, with blooming lotuses of stars, moon and sun in the blue lake of the sky.

[*Comment*: This one in which east and west take shape at the hours of sunrise and sunset, in front and behind. He shows colourful lotus-garden and so forth there.]

32. With the vines and leaves of rows of clouds arranged in diverse designs, puppet-images of celestial beings, *asuras*[12] and men drawn in the chambers of (the three worlds), its sky-walls white-washed with most brilliant light (of the sun and moon) (this world is a theatre).

33. In the very space, genius alone her theatre, young, innocent-looking, colouring all loci with whirling wheels[13] of the lights of consciousness alone; fervent in her play, this dancing girl, the triad of worlds, charming to the mind, is created by the sensual painter, *cittaka,*[14] the Mind.

[*Comment*: Now he presents the image of the world-trio[15] as the danseuse of the celestial ones, *devas*, as she is imagined as the puppet painted in the painting. The five verses starting from here present this imagery. She has been created as beautiful as this by the mind, which is naturally sensuous, lustful. She is created in the space

---

[12] *Asuras*, demonic beings opposed to celestial beings.

[13] Again here the spiritually suggestive choice of words: *cin-mātra-cakra-pari-rañjita-sarva-lokā*, having fully coloured and entertained all the worlds with the *cakras* (whirls or wheels) of pure consciousness alone.

[14] A play on words here. *Citraka* would be a painter; here this painter "this little mind" is *cittaka*.

[15] Play on feminine gender of the compound word *trilokī* (the world-trio) imagining it to be a dancing woman.

which is *Brahman*'s space (*brahmākāśa*), the very own Abode.[16] Genius (*pratibhā*), the intelligence that produces ever-new flashes at every blink of an eye is the very theatre hall (*raṅga*). In this dance hall, the lamp is the witness consciousness itself, flashing like whirling discs.[17] The worlds have been coloured, i.e. bathed, with the light of the adorning jewels that catch reflections, which are the *vr̥ttis*, functions of *buddhi*, and these are the worlds of the witness-consciousness acting as the lamp in the dancing-hall.]

34. The (slim) vine of whose (body and) limbs is the golden mountain, clouds the braids of her hair; looking at the worlds by moving her eyes, the moon and the sun, wearing for garments the scriptures that maintain control through (the instruction of) *dharma*, *artha* and *kāma*; the seven lower worlds (*pātālas*) her legs and the lofty earth her hips;

[*Comment*: The very *brahmāṇḍa*, the cosmic egg of *Brahman*, is golden, and this vine of limbs is her steady and firm body. As is said: the golden egg, shining with the light of a thousand suns (*Manu-Smr̥ti* 1.9). She wears the two (upper and lower) garments of *pravr̥tti* and *nivr̥tti*, the teachings concerning involvement in the world as well as withdrawal and renunciation. The seven lower worlds compare to the seven parts of her legs: thigh, inner thigh, knee, calf, ankle, feet and toes.]

35. She is strong, with four arms — Brahmā, Indra, Śiva and Viṣṇu;[18] her slim body has full quivering breasts covered

---

16 The source of the mind's lustfulness is suggested here by the word *svādhiṣṭhāna* (own abode) normally the name of the second centre of consciousness in *yoga*.

17 Exact wording here: flashing as *cakras* of the witness consciousness.

18 Brahmā, Viṣṇu, Śiva, the three aspects, creator, sustainer and dissolver,

→

with the bodice of harmony (*sattva*); the very earth enwrapped by beautiful snakes[19] is her lotus seat. She has the great middle world for her midriff, with its mountains for leafy drawings.

[*Comment*: Strong, with four arms, capable of producing whatever she wishes; her breasts are *viveka* discriminatory wisdom and *vairāgya*, dispassion; the snakes wrapping the earth are such as *śeṣa*; on her stomach, which is the middle world, this planet, various mountains are the decorative lines drawn with fragrant colours.]

36. The glances of her eyes stop the stirrings and shiftings of night's darkness, with stars for the thrill of her body-hair, lightning for rows of teeth; her bristling of hair, the (birth of) incomparable beings and fourteen worlds quivering; (wearing) the winds of dissolution for *kadamba*[20] flowers.

[*Comment*: The light of her eyes, which is the sun and the moon, stops the shifting of night's darkness as the sun goes round the central mountain Meru.[21] Lightning is her rows of teeth. The incomparable variety and differentiation of the fourteen worlds[22] together with all the beings is her horripilation (of wonder). Well known among those beings are the very mountain winds of dissolution. As

→ of the personal God. Indra, the king of paradise, not to be confused with *mokṣa* or *nirvāṇa* (spiritual liberation).

19 Suggestion of *mūlādhāra cakra* here.

20 *Neolmarckia cadamba*. A tree sacred to Kṛṣṇa in north India and to Pārvatī in south India. The tree under which the dalliances of Kṛṣṇa and Rādhā take place, and many other legends occur. Kṛṣṇa often wears garlands of *kadamba* flowers. An important flower for making fragrant essential oils, very popular in India.

21 Pivot of the earth.

22 The seven worlds above the earth and seven below.

a wind picks up many flowers, stamens and fragrances, so the knowledge concerning the dissolution,[23] becoming known to all the people, spreads the fragrances of wisdom, dispassion and right inclinations, which become the flower garlands hanging right down to the feet.]

37. Endowed with life, this wonder has been created in (empty) space, consisting of (empty) space alone. By mind, the maker of strange and durable pictures, expert in the art of refined painting (is created) this beautiful maiden, the world-trio, attractive (for her) many dalliances and graces.

[*Comment*: Endowed with life, i.e. the cosmic and individual *jīva*. The mind readily finds the raw materials of variegated propensities (*vāsanās*), desires and their acts, it is capable of immediately creating wondersome variety of paintings. Thus has (the mind) created this beautiful maiden, whose beauty has been described above, namely the world-trio (*trilokī*).]

In the Great Rāmāyaṇa of Vasiṣṭha, composed by Vālmīki as narrated by a messenger of *devas*, the Path to Liberation, Nirvāṇa Section in the Narrative of Arjuna end of the fifty-sixth (56th) canto.

---

[23] Dissolution here of the world-concept held in mind. Concept of the dissolution of the external world is irrelevant here. Dispassion (*vairāgya*) is the true dissolution.

Chapter VI

Arjuna's Achieving Rest

[*Comment*: The vision by which the mind quickly becomes clear of *vāsanās*, with self alone remaining in non-dual joy; that vision is being taught.]

The Lord said:

1. Know this to be the great wonder here, Arjuna,
   That first the mural is produced and then the wall rises.

   [*Comment*: Being helpful in loosening the propensities (*vāsanās*), here he describes first the previously shown vision of the wondersomeness of the world. On non-wall, i.e. without a support base, before detailing the forms and shapes of the world, the world-picture arises mentally. Thereafter, as included (in the same world-picture) there occurs the posterior arising of the vast expanse[1] of past and current universe being imagined as its support base.

   Or, this posterior arising (may be understood) as the vast expanse, the collective (*samaṣṭi*) as a grouping together of the individuated units (*vyaṣṭi*). This imagining of the collective dependent on the individuated.]

2. In a mural painted on a non-wall is seen the wall extended.

---

1 *Virāṭ*, the universe-body of Consciousness in the form of personal God of the universe. The concept is as ancient as *R̥gveda* 10.90.5. One of the most vivid descriptions of *virāṭ* is seen in *BhG*. Chapter 11, titled Virāṭ-Rūpa-Darśana, the Lord showing His *virāṭ* form to Arjuna. This is the most widely known description but there are many other texts detailing the philosophy of *virāṭ* as well as narrating the stores of the Divine Being showing His or Her *virāṭ* form.

Oh, strange is this magic! The gourd sank, the rock floated.

[*Comment*: Having the forms that are entirely impossible (of existence), this *māyā* and its impossibilities being contradictory — well known as such — he presents an example of such contradictions and impossibilities (of the universe). The kind of things that happen in dream and magic show.

3. When the three worlds consist of nothing but (empty) space, like a painting in the mind, then, in you is the very self of space. What is this arising of spaceness of I-ness?[2]

   [*Comment*: Leave alone the wonders of the world painting; in you, whose very self is consciousness-space in the void-self (*śūnyātman*), the rise of I-ness is even more strange.]

4. All (this universe) is void created in the void. The void dissolves in the void.

   In void, void is being experienced; in void the void is expanded.

   [*Comment*: If you see the universe, too, as (an extension of) consciousness-space, then also your view of (I-ness) is very strange.]

5. This long, groaning *saṁsāra* is coiled around by the rope of *vāsanā* like a string of long creation (process). By uncoiling the *vāsanā* alone is this uncoiled here, Arjuna.

   [*Comment*: Where there is this long wandering in the

[2] The word *vyoman* (space) is used in this verse three times. For the second occurrence the commentator translates as *cid-vyoman* (consciousnees-space) and makes it *śūnyātman* (the voide-self). The repeated occurrence of the word *śūnya* in *YV* may suggest Buddhist influence to some. However, the use of the words like *khaṁ* (space) to describe the nature of *Brahman* is very pre-Buddhistic even going back to *Yajurveda* (40.17) and elaborated upon in the Upaniṣads. Many scholars have written on the concept of *śūnya* in Vedic-Hindu thought and may be consulted for further investigations.

transmigratory (world), such a variegate picture-world is wrapped by the long stretching rope of *vāsanā*s. Like empty space coiled around by a rope is the consciousness space (*cid-ākāśa*) roped around by *vāsanā*.]

6. As a reflection in the mirror, so is this (world) itself in *Brahman*, beyond any cutting and breaking because of there being no other substratum.

   [*Comment*: Being difficult to break by means other than knowledge is also because of the strength of the substratum and not by itself.]

7. In *Brahman* there is no space other than *Brahman*. Then the cutting and breaking and so forth of sky[3] is what? How? Whose? By whom is (it) cut, by whom broken?

   [*Comment*: By the forces of the realization that there is no other but *Brahman*, one sees that all these operations, such as cutting and breaking (slaying of people), are impossible, and by this view all *vāsanā*s should be eradicated. So the stanza explains that since all the operations of cutting and bursting (the things) of the world that are subject to those operations, are only reflected in *Brahman*, and are nothing other than *Brahman* but the consciousness-space itself. Then who does the cutting and breaking of what, with what means, in what way, for the sake of what result and at what place or time? The view of the empirical behaviour of cutting is possible only if one is seeing (some entity) other than *Brahman*.]

8-10. Now through this knowledge, your *vāsanā*s have definitely disappeared. For one who is not free of *vāsanā*s, even though performing all righteous acts (*dharma*), even though knowing everything, still has his self very much in bondage, like a lion[4] in a cage — one whose ground of

---

[3] Same as space.

[4] The commentator gives the option of reading "parrot" instead of a lion.

consciousness has even a little seed of *vāsanās*, there grows a great forest of *saṁsāra*.

(But) the seed of *vāsanā*, totally burned with the fire of right knowledge of reality (and truth), which is then rooted and grown in the heart through constant practice (*abhyāsa*), then no longer grows.

[*Comment*: Even the minutest amount of *vāsanā* should not be maintained for it can produce a thousand undesirable results. It has to be burnt leaving no residue whatever.]

11. The burnt-out seed of *vāsanās* then no longer sinks into objects such as pain and pleasure, like a clear lotus leaf in the water.

[*Comment*: The mind whose seeds of *vāsanās* are burnt leaving no residue (does not sink into objects).]

12. Tranquil of self, all fears gone, having abandoned all the immeasurable expectations, blown out (*nirvāṇa*), all the great delusion of the mind melted away, having apprehended this purifying knowledge of accuracy completely, having rejected (the possibility of) killing (etc.), now abide in the self, a being of one, peace.[5]

[*Comment*: Summarizing the sequences of above given homilies, he establishes Arjuna in the state of freedom from *vāsanās*. O Arjuna, you have abandoned all your immeasurable expectations. Being so, you have apprehended my purifying and sacred teaching in the form of *Bhagavad-Gītā*. Your variety of great confusions of the mind has melted away. You have become free of the afflictions of (the thoughts of) killing kinsmen and so forth, now abide (as) peace-self, in a self free of *vāsanās*, your mind having melted away,[6] you solo, one, of the nature of pacific

---

5 *Eka-śānti-rūpaḥ*. Lit., one-peace-natured. Being one, being peace.

6 Leaving the mind behind is a fundamental precept of yoga. Its methods are taught in the branch known as *amanaska-yoga*.

Brahman as you have therefore extinguished (*nirvāṇa*)[7], i.e. attained transcendental supreme fulfilment.[8]

In the Great Rāmāyaṇa of Vasiṣṭha, composed by Vālmīki as narrated by a messenger of *devas*, the Path to Liberation, Nirvāṇa Section in the Narrative of Arjuna end of the fifty-seventh (57th) canto.

---

7 The difference between Buddhist *nirvāṇa* and the one espoused here is that Buddhism does not accept the final reality as *Brahman*.

8 *Nirvṛtti*. Bringing a project or creative process to its completeness, such as a potter's effort comes to *nir-vṛ* by having produced the pot he started out to make.

Chapter VII

The Fulfilment of Arjuna

[*Comment*: Here is being presented the possibility of elimination of *vāsanā*s together with nescience, through the awakening in the knowledge of reality. Thereby, too, Arjuna is being graced with fulfilment.[1]]

1. My delusion is gone; I have attained mindfulness by your grace, O infallible one;
   Now I remain free of doubt; I shall act according to your word.[2]
   Only by awakening to the essence (*tattva*) is the loss of *vāsanā*, together with ignorance, possible;
   Thereby the fulfilment of Arjuna is being narrated here.

   [*Comment*: O infallible one, the delusion (*moha*), ignorance together with *vāsanā*s, has vanished with your grace, i.e. by the teaching given out of compassion. The mindfulness that is realization has been attained, literally, memory of (my own being), the self, which is *svataḥ-siddha* (self-proved) requiring no external evidence; like someone who had been looking for a gold necklace he thought he had lost, but then remembered for it to be around his own neck. All my doubts concerning my being a doer of acts, such as killing of kinsmen, have gone, because of the loss of the seeds of all doubts. I shall do according to your word, both with regard to abiding in the (higher) reality, as well as the duties of empirical life as they arise.]

---

[1] *Kṛtārthatā*. To accomplish a purpose and to feel fulfilment thereby and to be grateful for it.

[2] *Bhagavad-Gītā* 18.23.

The Lord said:

2. If the *vṛttis* have been pacified clearly in the mind, with enlightenment, then know that *citta* (mind-field) having come to *sattva*, and definitely having arrived at pacification within.

   [*Comment*: Though Arjuna has expressed his fulfilment, the Lord wishes to strengthen his freedom from all the *vāsanās* together with their roots, with the help of enlightenment concerning the essence being taught: if all operations of the mind (*vṛttis*) have become tranquil in the heart, completely, through the knowledge of the essence, then the mind (*citta*) also, which consists of *vāsanās*, has come to rest. Know that personality (*sattva*) to have reached freedom from the *vāsanās*. As is said: "When all the desires that were dwelling in his heart have been relieved then the mortal becomes immortal and attains the *Brahman* here."[3]]

3-4. Here, that which without an object of consciousness is termed the Inward Conscious, which is completely liberated, leaving no remainder, i.e. All and in all directions. None of those of this world (and so on) finds that state, like a bird that leaves the earth and flies very high up in the sky.

   [*Comment*: All things that exist in the empirical world are essentially that *Brahman*, excluding nothing, which is the inwardly conscious experience in the *sāttvika* state with consciousness devoid of an object (defined in stanza 2). "Those of the world" such as (eyes and other senses) as well as ignorant people do not attain that high state, like that of a bird flown into the high place.]

5. Inwardly conscious, shining, pure, without ideation, know this self to be beyond (not being an object of experience); like something far from the eyes.

---

[3] *Bṛhadāraṇyaka Upaniṣad* 4.4.7; *Kaṭha Upaniṣad* 6.14.

[*Comment*: *Ābhāsa* (shining); i.e. the source of the illumination of the field consisting of the thirteen evolutes, such as the great elements and so on (presumably five subtle elements, five senses, *buddhi*, etc.).]

6. One's *vāsanā* cannot see that state which is pure, totally clear and excels all, the way people's sight (cannot see) minute atoms.

[*Comment*: For the realization of that, the essential effort is *nididhyāsana;* contemplation practised as part of cultivating in the mind (*bhāvanā*) what has been learned. It is totally clear because of being consciousness itself, pure because nothing attaches to it.]

7. To find which, all of these, jars, cloths, and things have failed and been eliminated, what can poor *vāsanā* do there, in the supreme state?

[*Comment*: Where gross and strong things such as jars and so on cannot reach, how can the poor, utterly subtle *vāsanā* get there?]

8. As a particle of ice dissolves upon reaching a volcano,[4] so ignorance (*avidyā*) dissolves upon attaining the pure consciousness-essence.

9. Where the poor little insignificant particle, the *vāsanā*, bound to experiences, and where the strong wind of the essence of consciousness, filling the entire network of the world.

[*Comment*: *Vāsanā*, minute like a dust particle in the wind (stands no chance before the strong wind of pure consciousness).]

10. This ignorance (*avidyā*) bringing forth changes and modifications of all kinds of forms, flashes around only as

---

[4] Literally "a fire-mountain".

long as this pure self has not been properly and completely known by the self.

11. All views of objects of perception have vanished, only the (transparent) purity has arisen, like that of a sky, in that state which is one's own self, filling and completing all.

[*Comment*: Filling, i.e. swallowing, everything into himself, into his own stomach (as everything is dissolved into the self).]

12. Having the form of all and whole configurations is that without configurations. With what, pray, can be compared that supreme reality beyond speech?

[*Comment*: All configurations, i.e. having the form of Fullness and Perfection itself, but devoid of the configurations of worldly existence.]

13. Therefore, give up this poisonous infection of objects and experiences (*viṣaya-viṣa-viṣūcikā*), throwing aside expertly the *vāsanā* of the stagnation in I-ness. By means of the secret antidote-*mantra*[5] of contemplation, become free of the worldly being,[6] a blessed lord, no (further) ground for fears and dangers.

[*Comment*: O Arjuna, give up, expertly, the *vāsanā* that dwells in the inner sense (*antaḥkaraṇa*) and consists of I-ness, as the cause of ever-involvement with worldly things. It is thus the poisonous infection of *viṣaya*s (objects and their experiences). It will be done through the application of a secret *mantra*, which consists of the prevention of the desired passion through the realization of the perfect self. (Thus) free of the bondage of *saṁsāra*, no longer a ground for all predicaments, by nature *abhaya*, devoid of all fears and dangers (know of yourself that) "I

5 This refers to controlling snakes and the cure of any poisoning by the power of *mantra*s.

6 *Vibhava*.

am the very Lord". This, at the end, is the statement of the essence of *Bhagavad-Gītā*.

Vasiṣṭha said:

14. When the Lord of the three worlds has thus spoken,
The son of Pāṇḍu, standing there before him, having entered silence for a moment,
Like a honey-bee on the tip of a blue lotus,
Will find these words to say:

Arjuna said:[7]

15. This my intelligence has reached the highest ascendance, Lord, with all the weight of grief completely dissolved by the words of you who are the master of the worlds, like a lily awakened by (the sun), the Lord of the day.

16. Thus saying, with all his doubts gone, (holding) his bow (named) Gāṇḍīva with the Lord Viṣṇu as his charioteer, Arjuna will rise and enter the play, the battle game.

17. He will turn the earth into a great river of blood, fast-flowing from wounded elephants, horses and charioteers.

He will darken the sky, covering the rays of the heavenly gem (the sun) with a thick sheet of dust and the spray of arrows, spreading together.[8]

In the Great Rāmāyaṇa of Vasiṣṭha, composed by Vālmīki as narrated by a messenger of *devas*, the Path to Liberation,
Nirvāṇa Section in the
Narrative of Arjuna
end of the fifty-eighth (58th) canto.
Here ends the Arjuna Narrative.

---

7 To bear in mind here, Vasiṣṭha is a *ṛṣi*, who is a *trikāla-darśin*, seer of three time division simultaneously. So he presents the future as past in "will find these words to say" in verse 14 but in introducing verse 15, it is "Arjuna said".

8 The commentary only paraphrases the words of the verse. It would be a tautology to present it here.

Appendix 1

Below we provide a list of verses, or fragments thereof, that occur both in *MB-BhG* and *YV-BhG*. Order of the sequence is according to the sequence in *MB-BhG*.[1] These are also listed by Karmarkar (1956: 63ff.) without showing the comparison between *YV-BhG* and *MB-BhG*.

Arjunopākhyāna from Yoga-Vāsiṣṭha and Bhagavad-Gītā from the Mahābhārata

मात्रास्पर्शा हि *कौन्तेय शीतोष्णसुखदुःखदाः।*
आगमापायिनोऽनित्यास्तांस्तितिक्षस्व भारत।।५४.२।।

mātrāsparśā hi *kaunteya śītoṣṇasukhaduḥkhadāḥ* ।
āgamāpāyino 'nityās tāṁs titikṣasva bhārata ।।54.2।।

मात्रास्पर्शास्तु कौन्तेय शीतोष्णसुखदुःखदाः।
आगमापायिनोऽनित्यास्तांस्तितिक्षस्व भारत।।२-१४।।

*mātrāsparśā*s tu *kaunteya śītoṣṇasukhaduḥkhadāḥ* ।
āgamāpāyino 'nityās tāṁs titikṣasva bhārata ।।2.14।।

नासतो विद्यते भावो नाभावो विद्यते सतः।
उभयोरपि दृष्टोऽन्तस्त्वनयोस्तत्त्वदर्शिभिः।।५४.७।।

nāsato vidyate bhāvo nābhāvo vidyate sataḥ ।
ubhayor api dr̥ṣṭo 'antas tv anayos tattvadarśibhiḥ ।।54.7।।

नासतो विद्यते भावो नाभावो विद्यते सतः।
उभयोरपि दृष्टोऽन्तस्त्वनयोस्तत्त्वदर्शिभिः।।२.१६।।

[1] We are gratedful to Sanjay Kumar for having collated this list and Pandit Chandramani for having further improved on it by italicizing the fragments of the verses for easy comparison.

nāsato vidyate bhāvo nābhāvo vidyate sataḥ |
ubhayor api dṛṣṭo 'antas tv anayos tattvadarśibhiḥ ||2.16||

य एनं वेत्ति हन्तारं यश्चैनं मन्यते हतम्।
उभौ तौ न विजानीतो नायं हन्ति न हन्यते।।५२.३७।।

ya enaṁ vetti hantāraṁ yaś cainaṁ manyate hatam |
ubhau tau na vijānīto nāyaṁ hanti na hanyate ||52.37||

य एनं वेत्ति हन्तारं यश्चैनं मन्यते हतम्।
उभौ तौ न विजानीतो नायं हन्ति न हन्यते।।२-१९।।

ya enaṁ vetti hantāraṁ yaś cainaṁ manyate hatam |
ubhau tau na vijānīto nāyaṁ hanti na hanyate ||2.19||

न जायते म्रियते वा कदाचिन्नायं भूत्वा भविता वा न भूयः।
अजो नित्यः शाश्वतोऽयं पुराणो न हन्यते हन्यमाने शरीरे।।५२.३६।।

na jāyate mriyate vā kadācin nāyaṁ bhūtvā bhavitā vā na bhūyaḥ |
ajo nityaḥ śāśvato 'yaṁ purāṇo na hanyate hanyamāne śarīre ||52.36||

न जायते म्रियते वा कदाचिन्नायं भूत्वा भविता वा न भूयः।
अजो नित्यः शाश्वतोऽयं पुराणो न हन्यते हन्यमाने शरीरे।।२-२०।।

na jāyate mriyate vā kadācin nāyaṁ bhūtvā bhavitā vā na bhūyaḥ |
ajo nityaḥ śāśvato 'yaṁ purāṇo na hanyate hanyamāne śarīre ||2.20||

आत्मैवेदं जगद्रूपं हन्यते *हन्ति* वात्र किम्।
शुभाशुभैर्जगद्दुःखैः किमस्यार्जुन लिप्यते।।५३.५५।।

ātmaivedaṁ jagadrūpaṁ hanyate *hanti* vātra kim |
śubhāśubhair jagadduḥkhaiḥ kimasyārjuna lipyate ||53.55||

वेदाविनाशिनं नित्यं य एनमजमव्ययम्।
कथं स पुरुषः पार्थ कं घातयति *हन्ति* कम्।।2-21।।

vedāvināśinaṁ nityaṁ ya enam ajam avyayam |
kathaṁ sa puruṣaḥ pārtha kaṁ ghātayati *hanti* kam ||2.21||

निर्द्वन्द्वो नित्यसत्त्वस्थो निर्योगक्षेम आत्मवान्।
यथाप्राप्तानुवर्ती त्वं भव भूषितभूतलः।।५४.३५।।

nirdvandvo nityasattvastho niryogakṣema ātmavān |
yathāprāptānuvartī tvaṁ bhava bhūṣitabhūtalaḥ ||54.35||

त्रैगुण्यविषया वेदा निस्त्रैगुण्यो भवार्जुन।
निर्द्वन्द्वो नित्यसत्त्वस्थो निर्योगक्षेम आत्मवान्।।२-४५।।

traiguṇyaviṣayā vedā nistraiguṇyo bhavārjuna |
nirdvandvo nityasattvastho niryogakṣema ātmavān ||2.45||

योगस्थः कुरु कर्माणि सङ्गं त्यक्त्वा धनञ्जय।।५३.१६।।

yogasthaḥ kuru karmāṇi saṅgaṁ tyaktvā dhanañjaya ||53.16||

मा कर्मफलहेतुर्भूर्मा ते सङ्गोऽस्त्वकर्मणि।
योगस्थः कुरु कर्माणि सङ्गं त्यक्त्वा धनञ्जय।।५४.२६।।

mā karmaphalahetur bhūr mā te saṅgo 'stv akarmaṇi |
yogasthaḥ kuru karmāṇi saṅgaṁ tyaktvā dhanañjaya ||54.26||

मा कर्मफलहेतुर्भूर्मा ते सङ्गोऽस्त्वकर्मणि।।२.४७।।
योगस्थः कुरु कर्माणि सङ्गं त्यक्त्वा धनञ्जय।।२.४८।।

mā karmaphala hetur bhūr mā te saṅgo 'stv akarmaṇi ||2.47||
yogasthaḥ kuru karmāṇi saṅgaṁ tyaktvā dhanañjaya ||2.48||

स्थिरां संस्थितिमायाति *कूर्मोऽङ्गानीव सर्वशः*।
*इन्द्रियाणीन्द्रियार्थेभ्यो*हृदि यस्य स्वभावतः।।५६.७।।

sthirāṁ saṁsthitamāyāti *kūrmo 'ṅgānīva sarvaśaḥ* |
indriyāṇīndriyārthebhyo hṛdi yasya svabhāvataḥ ||56.7||

यदा संहरते चायं *कूर्मोऽङ्गानीव सर्वशः*।
*इन्द्रियाणीन्द्रियार्थेभ्य*स्तस्य प्रज्ञा प्रतिष्ठिता।।२-५८।।

yadā saṁharate cāyaṁ *kūrmo 'ṅgānīva sarvaśaḥ* |
indriyāṇīndriyārthebhyas tasya prajñā pratiṣṭhitā ||2.58||

आपूर्यमाणमचलप्रतिष्ठं समुद्रमापः प्रविशन्ति यद्वत्।
तद्वत्कामा यं प्रविशन्ति सर्वे स शान्तिमाप्नोति न कामकामी ।।५४.३८।।

āpūryamāṇam acalapratiṣṭhaṁ samudram āpaḥ praviśanti yadvat |
tadvat kāmā yaṁ praviśanti sarve sa śāntim āpnoti na kāmakāmī ||54.38||

आपूर्यमाणमचलप्रतिष्ठं समुद्रमापः प्रविशन्ति यद्वत्।
तद्वत्कामा यं प्रविशन्ति सर्वे स शान्तिमाप्नोति न कामकामी ।।२.७०।।

āpūryamāṇam acalapratiṣṭhaṁ samudram āpaḥ praviśanti yadvat ।
tadvat kāmā yaṁ praviśanti sarve sa śāntim āpnoti na kāmakāmī ।।2.70।।

कर्मेन्द्रियाणि संयम्य य आस्ते मनसा स्मरन्।
इन्द्रियार्थान्विमूढात्मा मिथ्याचारः स उच्यते।।५३.३६।।

karmendriyāṇi saṁyamya ya āste manasā smaran ।
indriyārthān vimūḍhātmā mithyācāraḥ sa ucyate ।।54.36।।

कर्मेन्द्रियाणि संयम्य य आस्ते मनसा स्मरन्।
इन्द्रियार्थान्विमूढात्मा मिथ्याचारः स उच्यते।।३.६।।

karmendriyāṇi saṁyamya ya āste manasā smaran ।
indriyārthān vimūḍhātmā mithyācāraḥ sa ucyate ।।3.6।।

यस्त्विन्द्रियाणि मनसा नियम्यारभतेऽर्जुन।
कर्मेन्द्रियैः कर्मयोगमसक्तः स विशिष्यते।।५४.३७।।

yas tv indriyāṇi manasā niyamyārabhate 'rjuna ।
karmendriyaiḥ karmayogam asaktaḥ sa viśiṣyate ।।54.37।।

यस्त्विन्द्रियाणि मनसा नियम्यारभतेऽर्जुन।
कर्मेन्द्रियैः कर्मयोगमसक्तः स विशिष्यते।।३-७।।

yas tv indriyāṇi manasā niyamyārabhate 'rjuna ।
karmendriyaiḥ karmayogam asaktaḥ sa viśiṣyate ।।3.7।।

स्वात्मांशैः *क्रियमाणानि गुणैः कर्माणि* भागशः।
अहङ्कारविमूढात्मा कर्ताहमिति मन्यते।।५३.५।।

svātmāṁśaiḥ *kriyamāṇāni guṇaiḥ karmāṇi* bhāgaśaḥ ।
ahaṅkāravimūḍhātmā kartāham iti manyate ।।53.5।।

प्रकृतेः *क्रियमाणानि गुणैः कर्माणि* सर्वशः।
अहङ्कारविमूढात्मा कर्ताहमिति मन्यते।।३-२७।।

prakṛteḥ *kriyamāṇāni guṇaiḥ karmāṇi* sarvaśaḥ ।
ahaṅkāravimūḍhātmā kartāham iti manyate ।।3.27।।

अपि कुत्सितमप्यन्यदप्यधर्ममयक्रमम्।
श्रेष्ठं ते स्वं यथा कर्म तथेहामृतवान् भव॥५३.१४॥

api kutsitam apy anyad apy adharmamayakramam |
śreṣṭhaṁ te *svaṁ* yathā karma tathehāmṛtavān bhava ||53.14||

श्रेयान्स्वधर्मो विगुणः परधर्मात्स्वनुष्ठितात्।
स्वधर्मे निधनं श्रेयः परधर्मो भयावहः॥३.३५॥

śreyān svadharmo viguṇaḥ paradharmāt svanuṣṭhitāt |
*sva*dharme nidhanaṁ śreyaḥ paradharmo bhayāvahaḥ ||3.35||

कर्मण्यकर्म यः पश्येदकर्मणि च कर्म यः।
स बुद्धिमान्मनुष्येषु स चोक्तः *कृत्स्नकर्मकृत्*॥५४.२५॥

karmaṇy akarma yaḥ paśyed akarmaṇi ca karma yaḥ |
sa buddhimān manuṣyeṣu sa coktaḥ *kṛtsnakarmakṛt* ||54.25||

कर्मण्यकर्म यः पश्येदकर्मणि च कर्म यः।
स बुद्धिमान्मनुष्येषु स चोक्तः *कृत्स्नकर्मकृत्*॥४.१८॥

karmaṇy akarma yaḥ paśyed akarmaṇi ca karma yaḥ |
sa buddhimān manuṣyeṣu sa yuktaḥ *kṛtsnakarmakṛt* ||4.18||

यस्य सर्वे समारम्भाः कामसङ्कल्पवर्जिताः।
ज्ञानाग्निदग्धकर्माणं तमाहुः पण्डितं बुधाः॥५४.३३॥

yasya sarve samārambhāḥ kāmasaṅkalpavarjitāḥ |
jñānāgnidagdhakarmāṇaṁ tam āhuḥ paṇḍitaṁ budhāḥ ||54.33||

यस्य सर्वे समारम्भाः कामसङ्कल्पवर्जिताः।
ज्ञानाग्निदग्धकर्माणं तमाहुः पण्डितं बुधाः॥४.१९॥

yasya sarve samārambhāḥ kāmasaṅkalpavarjitāḥ |
jñānāgnidagdhakarmāṇaṁ tam āhuḥ paṇḍitaṁ budhāḥ ||4.19||

त्यक्त्वा कर्मफलासङ्गं नित्यतृप्तो निराश्रयः।
कर्मण्यभिप्रवृत्तोऽपि नैव किञ्चित्करोति सः॥५४.२८॥

tyaktvā karmaphalāsaṅgaṁ nityatṛpto nirāśrayaḥ |
karmaṇy abhipravṛtto 'pi naiva kiñcit karoti saḥ ||54.28||

त्यक्त्वा कर्मफलासङ्गं नित्यतृप्तो निराश्रयः।
कर्मण्यभिप्रवृत्तोऽपि नैव किञ्चित्करोति सः॥४.२०॥

tyaktvā karmaphalāsaṅgaṁ nityatṛpto nirāśrayaḥ।
karmaṇy abhipravṛtto 'pi naiva kiñcit karoti saḥ॥4.20॥

...... *कुर्वन्नपि न लिप्यते॥५३.१२॥*

...... *kurvann api na lipyate॥53.12॥*

योगयुक्तो विशुद्धात्मा विजितात्मा जितेन्द्रियः।
सर्वभूतात्मभूतात्मा *कुर्वन्नपि न लिप्यते॥५.७॥*

yogayukto viśuddhātmā vijitātmā jitendriyaḥ।
sarvabhūtātmabhūtātmā *kurvann api na lipyate॥5.7॥*

कायेन मनसा बुद्ध्या केवलैरिन्द्रियैरपि।
योगिनः कर्म कुर्वन्ति सङ्गं त्यक्त्वात्मशुद्धये॥५३.९॥

kāyena manasā buddhyā kevalair indriyair api।
yoginaḥ karma kurvanti saṅgaṁ tyaktvātmaśuddhaye॥53.9॥

कायेन मनसा बुद्ध्या केवलैरिन्द्रियैरपि।
योगिनः कर्म कुर्वन्ति सङ्गं त्यक्त्वात्मशुद्धये॥५.११॥

kāyena manasā buddhyā kevalair indriyair api।
yoginaḥ karma kurvanti saṅgaṁ tyaktvātmaśuddhaye॥5.11॥

सर्वभूतस्थमात्मानं सर्वभूतानि चात्मनि।
पश्य त्वं *योगयुक्तात्मा सर्वत्र समदर्शनः॥५३.४३॥*

sarvabhūtastham ātmānaṁ sarvabhūtāni cātmani।
paśya tvaṁ *yogayuktātmā sarvatra samadarśanaḥ॥53.43॥*

सर्वभूतस्थमात्मानं सर्वभूतानि चात्मनि।
ईक्षते *योगयुक्तात्मा सर्वत्र समदर्शनः॥६.२९॥*

sarvabhūtastham ātmānaṁ sarvabhūtāni cātmani।
īkṣate *yogayuktātmā sarvatra samadarśanaḥ॥6.29॥*

सर्वभूतस्थमात्मानं भजत्येकत्वमात्मनः।
सर्वथा वर्तमानोऽपि न स भूयोऽभिजायते॥५३.४४॥

*sarvabhūta*sthamātmānaṁ *bhajaty ekatvam* ātmanaḥ।
sarvathā vartamāno 'pi na sa bhūyo 'bhijāyate॥53.44॥

*सर्वभूत*स्थितं यो मां *भजत्येकत्व*मास्थितः।
सर्वथावर्तमानोऽपि स योगी मयि वर्तते॥६-३१॥

*sarvabhūta*sthitaṁ yo māṁ *bhajaty ekatvam* āsthitaḥ।
sarvathā vartamāno 'pi sa yogī mayi vartate॥6.31॥

नश्यत्सु न विनश्यन्तं *यः* पश्यति *स* पश्यति॥५३.५६॥

naśyatsu na vinaśyantaṁ *yaḥ* paśyati *sa* paśyati॥53.56॥

परस्तस्मात्तु भावोऽन्योऽव्यक्तोऽव्यक्तात्सनातनः।
यः स सर्वेषु भूतेषु *नश्यत्सु* न विनश्यति॥८.२०॥

paras tasmāt tu bhāvo 'nyo 'vyakto 'vyaktāt sanātanaḥ।
yaḥ sa sarveṣu bhūteṣu *naśyatsu na vinaśyati*॥8.20॥

यत्करोषि यदश्नासि यज्जुहोषि ददा*सि यत्*।
यत् करिष्यसि *कौन्तेय तदात्मे*ति स्थिरो भव॥५४.२२॥

yat karoṣi yad aśnāsi yaj juhoṣi dadāsi yat।
yat kariṣyasi *kaunteya tad* ātmeti sthiro bhava॥54.22॥

यत्करोषि यदश्नासि यज्जुहोषि ददा*सि यत्*।
यत्तपस्यसि *कौन्तेय तत्*कुरुष्व मदर्पणम्॥९.२७॥

yat karoṣi yad aśnāsi yaj juhoṣi dadāsi yat।
yat tapasyasi *kaunteya tat* kuruṣva madarpaṇam॥9.27॥

......
संन्यासयोगयुक्तात्मा ...॥५३.१९॥

......
saṁnyāsayogayuktātmā॥53.19॥

शुभाशुभफलैरेवं मोक्ष्यसे कर्मबन्धनैः।
संन्यासयोगयुक्तात्मा विमुक्तो मामुपैष्यसि॥९.२८॥

śubhāśubhaphalair evaṁ mokṣyase karmabandhanaiḥ।
saṁnyāsayogayuktātmā vimukto mām upaiṣyasi॥9.28॥

मन्मना भव मद्भक्तो मद्याजी मां नमस्कुरु।
मामेवैष्यसि युक्त्वैवमात्मानं मत्परायणः।।५३.३४।।

manmanā bhava madbhakto madyājī māṁ namaskuru |
mām evaiṣyasi yuktvaivam ātmānaṁ matparāyaṇaḥ ||53.34||

मन्मना भव मद्भक्तो मद्याजी मां नमस्कुरु।
मामेवैष्यसि युक्त्वैवमात्मानं मत्परायणः।।९.३४।।

manmanā bhava madbhakto madyājī māṁ namaskuru |
mām evaiṣyasi yuktvaivam ātmānaṁ matparāyaṇaḥ ||9.34||

भूय एव महाबाहो शृणु मे परमं वचः।
यत्तेऽहं प्रीयमाणाय वक्ष्यामि हितकाम्यया।।५४.१।।

bhūya eva mahābāho śr̥ṇu me paramaṁ vacaḥ |
yat te 'haṁ prīyamāṇāya vakṣyāmi hitakāmyayā ||54.1||

भूय एव महाबाहो शृणु मे परमं वचः।
यत्तेऽहं प्रीयमाणाय वक्ष्यामि हितकाम्यया।।१०.१।।

bhūya eva mahābāho śr̥ṇu me paramaṁ vacaḥ |
yat te 'haṁ prīyamāṇāya vakṣyāmi hitakāmyayā ||10.1||

निर्ममो निरहङ्कारः समदुःखसुखः क्षमी।
यः स कार्यमकार्यं वा कुर्वन्नपि न लिप्यते।।५३.१२।।

nirmamo nirahaṅkāraḥ samaduḥkhasukhaḥ kṣamī |
yaḥ sa kāryam akāryaṁ vā kurvann api na lipyate ||53.12||

अद्वेष्टा सर्वभूतानां मैत्रः करुण एव च।
निर्ममो निरहङ्कारः समदुःखसुखः क्षमी।।१२.१३।।

adveṣṭā sarvabhūtānāṁ maitraḥ karuṇa eva ca |
nirmamo nirahaṅkāraḥ samaduḥkhasukhaḥ kṣamī ||12.13||

सर्वथा वर्तमानोऽपि न स भूयोऽभिजायते।।५३.४४।।

sarvathā vartamāno 'pi na sa bhūyo 'bhijāyate ||53.44||

य एवं वेत्ति पुरुषं प्रकृतिं च गुणैः सह।
सर्वथा वर्तमानोऽपि न स भूयोऽभिजायते।।१३.२४।।

ya evaṁ vetti puruṣaṁ prakṛtiṁ ca guṇaiḥ saha |
sarvathā vartamāno 'pi na sa bhūyo 'bhijāyate ||13.24||

सर्वभूतस्थमात्मानं सर्वभूतानि चात्मनि।
यः पश्यति तथात्मानमकर्तारं स पश्यति।।५३.६०।।

sarvabhūtastham ātmānaṁ sarvabhūtāni cātmani |
yaḥ paśyati tathātmānam akartāraṁ sa paśyati ||53.60||

प्रकृत्यैव च कर्माणि क्रियमाणानि सर्वशः।
यः पश्यति तथात्मानमकर्तारं स पश्यति।।१३.३०।।

prakṛtyaiva ca karmāṇi kriyamāṇāni sarvaśaḥ |
yaḥ paśyati tathātmānam akartāraṁ sa paśyati ||13.30||

निर्मानमोहा जितसङ्गदोषा अध्यात्मनित्या विनिवृत्तकामाः।
द्वन्द्वैर्विमुक्ताः सुखदुःखसंज्ञैर्गच्छन्त्यमूढाः पदमव्ययं तत्।।५३.६६।।

nirmānamohā jitasaṅgadoṣā adhyātmanityā vinivṛttakāmāḥ |
dvandvair vimuktāḥ sukhaduḥkhasaṁjñair gacchanty amūḍhāḥ padam avyayaṁ tat ||53.66||

निर्मानमोहा जितसङ्गदोषा अध्यात्मनित्या विनिवृत्तकामाः।
द्वन्द्वैर्विमुक्ताः सुखदःखसंज्ञैर्गच्छन्त्यमूढाः पदमव्ययं तत्।।१५.५।।

nirmānamohā jitasaṅgadoṣā adhyātmanityā vinivṛttakāmāḥ |
dvandvair vimuktāḥ sukhaduḥkhasaṁjñair gacchanty amūḍhāḥ padam avyayaṁ tat ||15.5||

कर्मणां यः *फलत्यागस्तं* संन्यासं विदुर्बुधाः।।५३.३०।।

karmaṇāṁ yaḥ *phalatyāgas* taṁ saṁnyāsaṁ vidur budhāḥ ||53.30||

सर्वकर्म*फलत्याग*प्राहुस्त्यागं विचक्षणाः।।१८-२।।

sarvakarma*phalatyāgaṁ* prāhus tyāgaṁ vicakṣaṇāḥ ||18.2||

कर्मणां *यः फलत्यागस्तं* संन्यासं विदुर्बुधाः।।५३.३०।।

karmaṇāṁ *yaḥ phalatyāgas*taṁ saṁnyāsaṁ vidur budhāḥ ||53.30||

न हि देहभृता शक्यं त्यक्तुं कर्माण्यशेषतः।
यस्तु *कर्मफल*त्यागी स त्यागीत्यभिधीयते।।१८.११।।

na hi dehabhṛtā śakyaṁ tyaktuṁ karmāṇy aśeṣataḥ।
yas tu *karmaphala*tyāgī sa tyāgīty abhidhīyate।।18.11।।

यस्य नाहंकृतो भावो बुद्धिर्यस्य न लिप्यते।
हत्वाऽपि स इमाँल्लोकान्न हन्ति न निबध्यते।।५३.२।।

yasya nāhaṁkṛto bhāvo buddhir yasya na lipyate।
hatvā 'api sa imām̐l lokān na hanti na nibadhyate।।53.2।।

यस्य नाहंकृतो भावो बुद्धिर्यस्य न लिप्यते।
हत्वाऽपि स इमाँल्लोकान्न हन्ति न निबध्यते।।१८.१७।।

yasya nāhaṁkṛto bhāvo buddhir yasya na lipyate।
hatvā 'api sa imām̐l lokān na hanti na nibadhyate।।18.17।।

अपि कुत्सितमप्यन्यदप्यधर्ममयक्रमम्।
श्रेष्ठं ते *स्वं* यथा *कर्म* तथेहामृतवान् भव।।५३.१४।।

api kutsitam apy anyad apy adharmamayakramam।
śreṣṭhaṁ te *svaṁ* yathā *karma* tathehāmṛtavān bhava।।53.14।।

श्रेयान्स्वधर्मो विगुणः परधर्मात्स्वनुष्ठितात्।
*स्व*भावनियतं *कर्म* कुर्वन्नाप्नोति किल्बिषम्।।१८.४७।।

śreyān svadharmo viguṇaḥ paradharmāt svanuṣṭhitāt।
*sva*bhāvaniyataṁ *karma* kurvan nāpnoti kilbiṣam।।18.47।।

नष्टो मोहः स्मृतिर्लब्धा त्वत्प्रसादान्मयाच्युत।
स्थितोऽस्मि गतसन्देहः करिष्ये वचनं तव।।५८.१।।

naṣṭo mohaḥ smṛtir labdhā tvatprasādān mayācyuta।
sthito 'smi gatasaṁdehaḥ kariṣye vacanaṁ tava।।58.1।।

नष्टो मोहः स्मृतिर्लब्धा त्वत्प्रसादान्मयाच्युत।
स्थितोऽस्मि गतसन्देहः करिष्ये वचनं तव।।१८-७३।।

naṣṭo mohaḥ smṛtir labdhā tvatprasādān mayācyuta।
sthito 'smi gatasaṁdehaḥ kariṣye vacanaṁ tava।।18.73।।

Appendix 2

The verses below are quoted in Karmarkar (1956: 66). Appendix B from his manuscript B except for the final verse also from his manuscripts C, D and E. Some of the verses seem corrupted by the scribe hands and meanings are not absolutely clear. Our italics below, to show similarity with verses in *MB-BhG*.

After 54.4

> अनन्ते संनिवेशादौ हेम्नीव कटकादिका।
> *यं हि न व्यथयन्त्येते मात्रास्पर्शा* भ्रमात्मकाः।।

> *anante saṁniveśādau hemnīva kaṭakādikā* ।
> *yaṁ hi na vyathayantyete mātrāsparśā bhramātmakāḥ* ।।

> Upon immersion into the Infinite, like bracelet in gold, one whom these contacts with subtle sense objects do not cause suffering as they consist of only error. . . .

After 55.35

> वासनात्मानमेनं त्वं जीवं विद्धि शरीरकम्।
> स्ववासनात्मकैवास्य सत्तासंसृतिकारणम्।
> ध्रियते संसृतिस्तावद्यावत्स्फुरति वासना।।

> *vāsanātmānam enaṁ tvaṁ jīvaṁ viddhi śarīrakam* ।
> *svavāsanātmakaivāsya sattāsaṁsr̥tikāraṇam* ।
> *dhriyate saṁsr̥tis tāvad yāvat sphurati vāsanā* ।।

> Know thou this little insignificant body as individuate soul (*jīva*) to consist of past impressions and propensities therefrom (*vāsanās*). Its nature of being in its own *vāsanā*, it is the cause

and source of the transmigratory world of "existence". The transmigratory world is sustained only so long as the *vāsanā* flashes.

After 56.5

प्रवाहापतितं कर्म स्वमेव (क्रियते च?) यत्।
जीवन्मुक्तानुभावोऽसावजीवन्मुक्ततान्यथा।।

pravāhāpatitaṁ karma svameva (kriyate ca?) yat ।
jīvanmuktānubhāvo 'sāvajīvanmuktatānyathā ।।

The action is undertaken as it comes in the course of the flow. Such is the majesty of the one liberated-while-living (*jīvan-mukta*) that he (behaves) like the non-liberated-while-living.

After 56.7

(इदं कर्म?) त्यजामीदमाश्रयामीत्यनिर्मलम्।
मूढस्य मनसो रूपं ज्ञमनस्कसमा स्थितिः।।

(idaṁ karma?) tyajāmīdam āśrayāmīty anirmalam ।
mūḍhasya manaso rūpaṁ jñamanaskasamā sthitiḥ ।।

I abandon (this act) or resort to it — such non-immaculate (indulgences). Form belongs to a stupefied mind. The station of a knowing and well-cultivated mind is balanced and even.

चिन्मात्रे वितते तन्तौ दृढे स्रगिव संस्थितम्।
सदसद्ग्रथितं विश्वं विश्वाङ्गे विश्वकर्मणि।।

cinmātre vitate tantau dṛḍhe sragiva saṁsthitam ।
sadasadgrathitaṁ viśvaṁ viśvāṅge viśvakarmaṇi ।।

It is stabilized well like a necklace woven in a strong well-fastened thread that is the extended consciousness-alone (*cin-mātra*). The universe is strung in being and non-being, in the organs of the universe and in universe-acts.

प्रसारिते प्रसरति स्वन्तर्धिर्याति संवृते।
विचित्ररचनाजालमनन्यश्चिद्वितानके।।

prasārite prasarati svantardhiryāti saṁvṛte ।
vicitraracanājālam ananyaś cidvitānake ।।

Expanded, it stretches out; contracted it goes into concealment within itself. The variegated network of mind's fancies is (in essence) non-other in the canopy of consciousness.

अनन्यमप्यन्यदिव साङ्गरूपमनङ्गवत्।
चित्रं वितानक इव स्थितं जगदिदं चिति।।

ananyam apy anyad iva sāṅgarūpam anaṅgavat ।
citraṁ vitānaka iva sthitaṁ jagad idaṁ citi ।।

Though non-other it [becomes], as it were, other; a form with organs [becomes] like one with non-organs; like a painting [hanging] in a canopy, this universe is sustained in consciousness.

यथैवारचितं चित्रं स्थितं चित्रकृदेहिते।
तथा जातमजातं च विश्वं संस्थितमात्मनि।
यथा स्फुरति कर्तव्यं चित्रं चित्रकृतिश्चिति।।

yathaivāracitaṁ citraṁ sthitaṁ citrakṛdehite ।
tathā jātam ajātaṁ ca viśvaṁ saṁsthitam ātmani ।
yathā sphurati kartavyaṁ citraṁ citrakṛtiś citi ।।

Like a painting not formed stays in the (?intention) of the painter. Similarly, born or unborn universe remains sustained in self (*ātman*) the way the intended painting flashes in the consciousness of the painter.

After 57.7

ब्रह्मताब्रह्मतापूरे जले जलमिव स्फुरत्।
स्थिता समसमा व्योम निर्मला शान्तमात्मनि।।
वास्यवासकभावोतो मनागपि न भिद्यते।

brahmatābrahmatāpūre jale jalam iva sphurat ।

sthitā samasamā vyoma nirmalā śāntamātmani ||
vāsyavāsakabhāvoto manāg api na bhidyate |

In the fullness of *Brahman*-ness in *Brahman*-ness, like water splashing in water, the balanced evenness, an immaculate space, pacific, is sustained in stillness in the self (*ātman*). There is not the slightest difference beween the perfume-suffuser and the suffused.[1]

No location cited (somewhere in Ch. 52?)

धृतराष्ट्रसुतैः सार्द्धं संग्रामेऽत्यन्तदारुणे।
उपैष्यन्त्यर्जुनं नैते योद्धुं तद्बान्धवोऽखिलाः।।

dhr̥tarāṣṭrasutaiḥ sārddhaṁ saṁgrāme 'tyantadāruṇe |
upaiṣyanty arjunaṁ naite yoddhuṁ tadbandhavo 'khilāḥ ||

In the very terrible war with the sons of Dhr̥tarāṣṭra, all these kinsmen will gather to fight against Arjuna.

1 As in Śaṅkara's commentary on the first verse of *Īśa Upaniṣad*, the universe is suffused as by a perfume, by the Lord.

Bibliography

Abhinanda and K. Narayanaswami Aiyar, *Laghu-Yoga-Vāsiṣṭha*, Madras: Adyar Library and Research Centre, 1971.

Abhinanda, Vāsudeva Lakṣmaṇa Paṇaśīkara, and Ātmasukha, *Laghu-Yoga-Vāsiṣṭha*, Vāsiṣṭha-candrikā-vyākhyā-sahitaḥ / [Ātmasukha]. Mumbayyām: Nirṇayasāgarākhyamudrṇālaya, 1937.

Atreya, B.L. and A.B. Dhruva, *The Vāsiṣṭha-darśanam*, Benares: Banaras Hindu University, 1936.

Atreya, B.L., *Deification of Man: Its Methods and Stages According to the Yoga-Vāsiṣṭha*, Moradabad: Darshana Printers, 1963.

———, *The Vision and the Way of Vasiṣṭha = Vāsiṣṭha-darśanam*, Madras: Indian Heritage Trust, 1993.

———, *The Yoga-Vāsiṣṭha and Its Philosophy*, Benares: Printed by Rameshwar Pathak, at the Tara Printing Works, 1939 (3rd edn.), Moradabad: Darshana Printers, 1966.

———, *Yoga-Vāsiṣṭha and Modern Thought*, or, *Agreement of the East and the West on Fundamental Problems*, Benares: Lectures delivered under the auspices of the Kashi Tattva Sabha, Theosophical Society (Second Series, VI-X), 1934; (Reprint) Benares: The Indian Book Shop, 1954.

———, *The Philosophy of the Yoga-Vāsiṣṭha*, Adyar, Madras: The Theosophical Publishing House, 1936.

Bhāskarakaṇṭha's Ṭīkā (commentary) on Abhinavagupta's Īśvara-Pratyabhijñā-Vimarśinī, ed. Ramachandra Dvivedi et al., Delhi: Motilal Banarsidass, 1986.

Bhāskarakaṇṭha, Jürgen Hanneder, and Walter Slaje, *Mokṣopāya-ṭīkā: A Commentary on the Earliest Available Recension of the Yoga-Vāsiṣṭha*, 1, Vairāgya-prakaraṇam, Aachen: Shaker, 2002.

Cakravartī, Kṣitīśa Candra, *Gītāmṛta: (Śāṅkara bhāṣya evaṁ Yoga-Vāsiṣṭha anusāra pramāṇa tātparya Hindī bhāṣā ṭīkā*), Vārāṇasī [u.a.]: Hindī Sāhitya Kuṭīra [u.a.], 1986.

Chapple, Christopher Key, Karam *and Creativity*, Albany, NY: State University of New York Press, 1986.

Gauḍa, Abhinanda, and Peter Thomi, *Yoga-Vāsiṣṭha-Sāra*, Wichtrach: Institut für Indologie Wichtrach, 1999.

Guptā, Rādhā, *Bhāratīya-darśana meṁ Yoga-Vāsiṣṭha kā sthāna*, Dillī: Parimala Pablikeśansa, 2002.

Hanneder, Jürgen (ed.), *Mokṣopāya, Yoga-Vāsiṣṭha and Related Texts*, Aachen: Shaker Verlag, 2005.

Hanneder, Jürgen and Walter Slaje, *Bhāskarakaṇṭha's Mokṣopāya-ṭīkā*, Part 1: Vairāgya-prakaraṇam, Aachen: Shaker Verlag, 2002.

Hanneder, Jürgen, Peter Stephan and Stanislav Jager, *Bhāskarakaṇṭha's Mokṣopāya-ṭīkā*, Part 2: Utpatti-prakaraṇam, Wiesbaden: Harrassowitz Verlag, 2011.

Hanneder, Jürgen, *Studies on the Mokṣopāya*, Wiesbaden: Harrassowitz, 2006.

Jnanananda Bharati, *The Essence of Yoga-Vasishtha* (tr. Samvid), Chennai: Samata Books, 1982.

Junejā, Lalitā Kumārī, *Yoga-Vāsiṣṭha meṁ Mukta kā Svarūpa*, Dillī: Vidyānidhi Prakāśana, 2010.

Karmarkar, R.D., *Arjunopākhyāna*, Poona: R.N. Dandekar at the Bhandarkar Oriental Research Institute, 1956.

Krause-Stinner, Susanne, *Mokṣopāya: Vairāgya-prakaraṇam, Mumukṣu-vyavahāra-prakaraṇam*, vol. 1, Wiesbaden: Harrassowitz Verlag, 2011.

Kuppuswamy, B., *The Quintessence of Yoga-Vāsiṣṭha*, Bangalore: C.S. Gupta, 1978.

Larson, Gerald James, and Ram Shankar Bhattacharya, *Yoga: India's Philosophy of Meditation*, Delhi: Motilal Banarsidass, 2008.

Lo Turco, Bruno, *Il Mokshopaya*, Rome: Doctoral Thesis, 1998.

———, *Mokṣopāya-ṭīkā of Bhāskarakaṇṭha, "The Fragments of the Nirvāṇa-prakaraṇa"*, Part 1, Wittenberg: Universitätsverlag Halle, 2011.

The Mahābhārata, The Ādi-parvan, Part 1, Critical Edition, ed. Vishnu S. Sukthankar, S.K. Belvalkar, Bhandarkar Oriental Research Institute, Pune, 1997.

Mainkar, T.G., *The Vasishtha Ramayana: A Study*, New Delhi: Meharchand Lachhmandas, 1977.

Mitra, Vihārilāl, *The Yoga-Vāsiṣṭha-Mahārāmāyṇa of Vālmīki*, Varanasi: Bharatiya Pub. House, 1976.

O' Flaherty, Wendy Doniger, *Dreams, Illusion and Other Realities*, Delhi [u.a.]: Motilal Banarsidass, 1987.

Pandey, K.C., *Abhinavagupta: An Historical and Philosophical Study*, Varanasi: Chaukhamba Amarabharati Prakashan (3rd edn.), 2000.

Pansikar, Wasudeva Laxmana Sastri, *The Yoga-Vāsiṣṭha of Vālmīki: With the Commentary Vāsiṣṭha-Mahārāmāyaṇa-Tātparya-Prakāśa*, New Delhi: Munshiram Manoharlal, 1981.

Prajñānanda, Prakhara, *Yoga-Vāsiṣṭha-Sāra: Sarala Hindī Vyākhyā*, Vārāṇasī: Caukhambā Saṁskṛta Saṁsthāna, 2009.

Sahadeva, Mañjulā (ed.), *Yoga-Vāsiṣṭha Mahārāmāyaṇa, A Perspective*: research papers presented in the International seminar held during 26-28 February 2003, Patiala: Maharshi Valmiki Chair, Punjabi University, 2004.

Schotsman, Irma, *Twenty-two Laghu-Yoga-Vāsiṣṭha Selections*, Sanskrit text with word-by-word translation into English, Delhi: Nag Publishers, 2005.

Sinhā, Udaya Nārāyaṇa, Lakhnau: Akhila Bhāratīya Samskṛta Pariṣad, 2001.

Slaje, Walter, *Bhāskarakaṇṭha's Mokṣopāya-ṭīkā "Die Fragmente des 4. (Sthiti-) prakaraṇa"*, Aachen: Shaker Verlag, 2002.

———, *Vom Mokṣopāya-śāstra zum Yoga-Vāsiṣṭha-mahārāmāyaṇa*, Wien: Österreichischen Akademie der Wissenschaften, 1994.

Tejomayananda, *Yoga-Vāsiṣṭha Sāra Saṁgrahaḥ = The Essence of Yoga Vāsiṣṭha*, Mumbai: Chinmaya Publications, 1998.

Vālmīki and Vāsudeva Lakṣmaṇa Paṇaśīkara, *The Yoga-Vāsiṣṭha*, with the commentary *Vāsiṣṭha-Mahā-Rāmāyaṇa-Tātparya-Prakāśa*, 2, Containing Nirvāṇa-Pūrvārdha and Uttarārdha, S. 774-1572, Delhi [u.a.]: Motilal Banarsidass, 1984.

———, *Vairāgya, Mumukṣu, Utpatti, Sthiti and Upaśama*, Bombay: Jāwajā, 1918.

Vālmīki, Pranav Tirtha, and Chidananda Tirtha, *The Yoga-Vāsiṣṭha Rāmāyaṇa, or The Last Word*, Chiang Mai: s.n., 2007.

Vālmīki, *The Yoga-Vāsiṣṭha Mahārāmāyaṇa*, Calcutta: Prajna Publications, 1991.

Venkatesananda and Christopher Key Chapple, *The Concise Yoga-Vāsiṣṭha*. Albany, N.Y.: State University of New York Press, 1984.

Venkatesananda, *Vasiṣṭha's Yoga*, Albany, N.Y.: State University of New York Press, 1993.

Other Bibliographies

The above bibliography will be an incomplete resource without reference to the comprehensive bibliographies found in the following above-cited works:

Atreya (1936): 28-35

Slaje (1994): 11-28

Lo Turco (1998): 248-80

Hanneder and Slaje (2002): 25-27

Slaje (2002): 5-8

Hanneder (2005): 144-53

Krause-Stinner (2011): lxviii-lxxiii

Lo Turco (2011): 7-10

Manuscripts

Atreya (1936): 35-40

Karmarkar (1956): i-iii

Hanneder (2005): 139-40

Index